I0152384

NER
press

The Real Nature of Religion

The Prophets Hosea and Jonah by Raphael

The Real Nature
of Religion

Rebecca Bynum

Published by New English Review Press
a subsidiary of World Encounter Institute
PO Box 158397
Nashville, Tennessee 37215
&
27 Old Gloucester Street
London, England, WC1N 3AX

Cover Design by Kendra Mallock

Cover photograph: Sombrero Galaxy in infrared light (Hubble Space Telescope and Spitzer Space Telescope)
Credit: NASA/JPL-Caltech and The Hubble Heritage Team (STScI/AURA)

ISBN: 978-0-9916521-5-0

First Edition

NEW ENGLISH REVIEW PRESS
newenglishreview.org

"Of all the dispositions and habits, which lead to political prosperity, Religion and Morality are indispensable supports. In vain would that man claim the tribute of Patriotism, who should labor to subvert these great pillars of human happiness, these firmest props of the duties of Men and Citizens. The mere Politician, equally with the pious man, ought to respect and to cherish them. A volume could not trace all their connections with private and public felicity. Let it simply be asked, Where is the security for property, for reputation, for life, if the sense of religious obligation desert the oaths, which are the instruments of investigation in Courts of Justice? And let us with caution indulge the supposition, that morality can be maintained without religion. Whatever may be conceded to the influence of refined education on minds of peculiar structure, reason and experience both forbid us to expect, that national morality can prevail in exclusion of religious principle."

— George Washington, *Farewell Address*, 1796

Contents

Acknowledgements

I would like to thank my husband, Hal Bynum, for his undying help and support. I would also like to thank the board members of World Encounter Institute, Hugh Fitzgerald, Ibn Warraq, Jerry Gordon, Richard L. Rubenstein, Roy Bishko and Julia Raffety, for standing firmly though all the ups and downs of *New English Review*. I would also like to thank all our authors and contributors who have patiently endured my questions, edits (questionable or otherwise) and complaints, especially Anthony Daniels, Geoffrey Clarfield and G. Murphy Donovan. I would also like to thank Esmerelda Weatherwax for bravely taking on the responsibility of our London office and Mary Jackson whose wit and humor never fails to raise all our spirits. And finally, to my many teachers who never wavered in their mission to help me carry out the tasks assigned, thank you.

Introduction

SINCE THE PUBLICATION of my last book, *Allah is Dead: Why Islam is Not a Religion* in 2011, I have been concentrating on the problem of what religion really is, for I have become convinced that in our modern secular world, we have largely forgotten the true nature of religion.

Though religion contains theology, it is more than theology. It concerns ethics and morality, but is more than ethics and morality. It ponders cosmology and man's place in the totality of creation, but it is more than cosmology. Religion often involves ritual and veneration for tradition, but it is more than ritual and tradition. All of these things contain and support religion, but they are not religion; they constitute the forms of religion. These things are only the riverbed, religion is the river. Those who point to a set of beliefs and declare them to be the length and breadth of a religion could not be more mistaken.

In the development of religion, religious experience invariably comes first; the effort to explain the experience, to fit it into an earlier mold or to create a new religious form, comes second. Experience always precedes and shapes what may afterwards become doctrine or ritual. Religious experience extends back to the very beginning of humanity, when God touched man and made him more than an animal; then man touched God and experienced the urge to worship and the desire to grasp and retain the divine presence.

Religion is the pursuit of total reality. It is not content with describing partial reality, that is to say, material reality or psychological reality, nor is it content with metaphysical speculation alone. Religion derives from an awareness which unites man's inner and outer worlds in a blaze of superb discernment. With the religious experience, existence begins to make sense. One feels at home in the universe, at home in one's own skin, and the attainment of that inner comfort and peace, which passes understanding, finally becomes possible. When witnessed in another person, the religious life is unmistakable. The superbly integrated personality is invariably a religious one, despite protests to the contrary by the militant atheist crowd.

Religion can never be completely codified or reduced to a doctrine or set of beliefs, though many men have tried. Religion is rooted in experience and the fact is, every person's religious experience is different. It cannot be replicated in a laboratory. It cannot be so fully explained as to be transferred to another person. Religion is not experienced by the senses or in the mind alone. The religious experience is total, involving all levels of being at once. As the search for total reality, religion is an all or nothing affair.

The religious seeker differs from the scientist. He is not seeking the answer to a question; he is seeking the answer to all questioning, life's ultimate fulfillment. The religious seeker perceives the current of reality runs in only two directions, toward the ultimate reality of God, or away from him and toward unreality, ultimately culminating in self-extinction.

Many people tire along the way and find a comfortable place to rest, accepting a doctrine or form of religion which offers stability and some degree of safety from confusion. The true religious pioneer, however, is not satisfied with that. He will go through any storm, any test and any trial to find the Truth. He will swim against the current of his time. He will fight the moral battle of the ages alone if need be. He will find what is needed for the journey and he will follow the divine beckoning wheresoever it may lead.

I am convinced that today we are witnessing the culmination of a centuries old struggle between industry and militarism. The advocates of industry hold that in our present time, industry does a better job in providing mankind with those things which the martial fields once supplied. Industry fosters leadership and a degree of hierarchy based on merit, provides challenge and adventure through competition, even the thrill of victory and the agony of defeat in the great moral drama of life. Industry gives man a worthy outlet for his creative impulses. In this world, war is still a necessary evil, for self-defense is yet required. The Western world, however, no longer desires military expansion; instead, it wants the expansion of trade. It seeks to create wealth, it no longer desires to confiscate it.

The belief system of Islam is currently the final bastion sustaining war and conquest as a religious obligation. The Western world has abandoned anything approaching that kind of reasoning. That thinking lies buried in the terrible destruction of the great world wars of the twentieth century. Expansionist wars have long since lost their glamour. Instead, the Western world requires peace and stability in order to advance through industry, commerce and technology.

Territorial conquest is a thing of the past because it is no longer required in order to bring increased prosperity to the people of a nation. War that once promised glory in battle is now only indiscriminate mass bloodshed. As Robert E. Lee once said, "It is well that war is so terrible, otherwise we should grow too fond of it."

Our Western world is trying valiantly to transcend war, yet is being reluctantly dragged back into it by the religion of war, a religion which thrives on hatred and fear. This is undoubtedly a struggle not only between levels of civilization, but also between levels of spiritual and moral reality—religious reality.

Our brave new world of technology and industry desperately needs a new and greater religious vision in order to create and sustain that center of unity and integration, without which it is apt to fly apart from the great centrifugal force it has created within. Our world also needs to articulate the moral vision with which it must confront our implacable enemy and *his* vision of reality.

I do not presume to know what that greater vision will be, but I do know that it is absolutely necessary and I also know that it must be rooted in individual religious experience. I will begin this study with an exploration of the various distortions of religion running through the currents in our modern world, most notably, repentance, tolerance and forgiveness, and then move on to how the misunderstanding of religion has led to a faulty analysis of Islam. Finally, I will attempt to describe and explain the reality of religious experience as the search for total reality, for Truth, and the yearning for absolute Goodness, profound Beauty and the thrill of experiencing God's Love.

We may not yet see the way forward, but through faith, we can know it is there.

- 1 -
Repentance Revisited

*Verily I say unto you, inasmuch as ye have done it
unto one of the least of these my brethren, ye have
done it unto me.*

— Matthew 25:40

O NE OF THE most disturbing aspects of observing
the general abandonment of religion and morality in our society, is the all too common spectacle of some
public figure, who, having behaved in an immoral fashion,
must then go through thoroughly predictable motions, undoubtedly originating in a public relations office somewhere,
which requires a person to a) make a public confession of his
unseemly acts (and don't leave out the details), and/or b) to
toddle off to some rehab clinic for "therapy," thereby imply-
ing that his moral failings were not actually moral failings at
all, but the result of disease, that is, some psychic or physical (usually an ill-defined "genetic") disorder. Alcoholism, to
be sure, contains elements of both: a genetic predisposition
coupled with free will action. Alcoholism definitely cannot
be said to be purely the result of moral failure, but the al-

coholism model has now seemingly been extended to the entire moral realm.

Morality originates in the mind and free will of the actor. It is the act of choosing between levels of value. Illness is the result of some psychological or bodily malfunction and usually has very little to do with free will. These two concepts are opposed and yet modern man tries to reconcile them and make them one. Thus, the rehab visit is taken as an act of contrition, which it is not.

Philandering, for example, is no longer thought to be the result of inattention to civilized self-control, but rather the result of a deep genetically-determined and overwhelming evolutionary need to procreate and to procreate as much and as often as possible. It was the selfish gene, not the selfish man who committed adultery, had sex with the hotel maid or flashed young girls by picture phone. If men are genetically impelled to behave like brutes, because they are, in fact, nothing more than brutes, well, who can blame them?

Furthermore, if there is no meaning to life other than what pleasure can be snatched during one's own brief hour on earth, are we then correct in censuring our "best and brightest" for seeking after this form of meaning? Aren't those who continue to insist that marriage be kept as a unique institution between one man and one woman the modern equivalent of the Victorian bluestocking lecturing the flapper? Doesn't progress demand the continual lowering of moral standards and doesn't scientific progression promote the abandonment of morality altogether?

Much of the condemnation of Anthony Weiner, for example, came down to a question of his judgment, rather than the conduct itself even though it was undoubtedly demeaning to the office. How long can we continue to engage in moral outrage when the basis for morality, religious belief and belief in the reality of value, has all but disappeared and is now nothing but a pale ghost haunting the twilight of the civilization it once nurtured—a father's picture on the dresser—both seen and unseen.

As was the case with John Edwards, the Weiner scandal spawned cubicles full of junior attorneys combing through the files for a technicality to indict Weiner with, some use of public facilities or funds in his phone flashing escapades that could constitute breach of office or, even better, an indictable offense. Weiner himself, while embarrassed (at least I hope he was embarrassed), didn't seem to see how his personal and private behavior should be the subject of public scrutiny let alone grounds for removal from office. Upon his resignation, he characterized the public disclosure of his behavior as a "distraction" that has prevented him from performing his public duty.

I am not entirely unsympathetic with this view. Many a great and good man has had personal moral failings of one sort or another, in fact, most have. It is certainly difficult to believe anyone but the most egotistical would want to run for office these days when a candidate's life is bound to be picked over in minute and often embarrassing detail. This may begin to explain the general decline in political leadership which has accelerated since the television age began, but part of it may also be explained by the decline into ridicule of old fashioned character building concepts like those of sin and repentance. The modern game of spirituality is played by moving one's piece straight to the self-forgiveness square. We are our own gods now and are endowed with the divine power to forgive sin. A greater trivialization of sin, and indeed life itself, cannot be imagined.

To sin is to knowingly rebel against the true and the right; to be fully cognizant that an action is wrong and would cause great suffering to others (were it to be revealed) and yet to persist in that action out of purely selfish motives:

this is sin. For those who have developed a relationship with the person of God, it is the conscious disloyalty to him and awareness of a break in one's relationship with him that constitutes sin. Naturally, sin is a destroyer of self-respect and yet the turning away from sin and the return to righteousness is rare without the sinner experiencing the full effects of the pain and suffering his actions have caused.

Though the concept of repentance may bring to mind a picture of Medieval monks scourging themselves, repentance is actually a much needed and practical response to sin. Marriages and careers may be completely destroyed today and still repentance is off the table. Instead, denial is bolstered by the idea that the selfish action is only the proximate cause of disaster (the ultimate cause was a disease which caused some dysfunction), thus removing or downplaying the selfish motives and selfish actions (along with the need to rectify them), from the picture. We are not sufficient to stand, our genes or hormones, or childhood, or diet or something other than our own free will choice, causes us to fall.

Repentance is a pure act of free will born of the desire to repair relations with God and to bring one's life back under his auspices. Indeed, it is the mechanism that allows escape from the slavery to lower appetites, which, while thrilling, do not compare to the thrill and comfort of divine love. Like prayer and charity, repentance is most effective when done in private, as part of one's personal understanding of God's character and his will. It is part of the process of regaining self-respect, walking back from the brink (or the ashes) of self-destruction. It is not a process that is done in a two week retreat that reinforces the idea that nothing is really anyone's fault to begin with. The act of repentance is the supreme act of taking responsibility and involves making amends to those who have been wronged. It is the active turning away from self and toward God; the return to the divine embrace and the act of grateful acceptance of divine forgiveness. Repentance creates profound psychological effects and is the one true elevator of self-esteem because it restores self-honesty.

It certainly causes a great change in the soul, such that if the sin is revisited, extreme anguish is experienced, such as that depicted so well by Victor Hugo in *Les Misérables*. In the story, Jean Valjean experienced that "strange phenomenon, and one which was possible only in the situation in which he found himself,—in stealing the money from that child, he had done a thing of which he was no longer capable." For he had willed in himself to follow the better way (after the old priest had ransomed his soul with the silver candlesticks), and therefore became conscious of the evil of his deed and was disgusted by it. Henceforth, he found himself living on a higher spiritual plane and from that vantage point, the reality of sin was clearly visible.

One has the impression that Anthony Weiner is not yet conscious of the evil in his deeds and is still uncomprehending of society's demand for repentance. But how can we demand repentance where there is no comprehension of the reality of sin? We are rapidlyly moving into a world where legality and morality are equivalent as they are in Islam. Despite the old maxim that one "cannot legislate morality" there are many, many people who would do just that. My own state of Tennessee has passed an anti-bullying bill that covers any internet posting which "causes emotional distress," similar to the hate speech laws in effect in Europe. This particular law is unlikely to stand the test of constitutionality, but that won't prevent more laws of this type being passed which attempt to force people to be civil to one another. There is no end to it once values are perceived to be a figment of the imagination, and there is nothing to live up to. All that is left is to live in avoidance of civil penalties, which is no life at all.

There is no greater indicator that Western culture has lost its way than these attempts to fuse morality and legality, or to substitute the latter for the former. The moral ground is giving way and so legality seems more solid, but that is the way of chaos and destruction. It is the sounding of the death knell of the West.

- 2 -
Can We Withstand the Divine Gaze?

I indeed baptize you with water unto repentance,
but he that cometh after me is mightier than I, whose
shoes I am not worthy to bear: he shall baptize you
with the Holy Ghost, and with fire.
— John the Baptist (Matthew 3:11)

THOSE WHO WERE baptized by John were not doing it for themselves alone but for the Jewish nation as a whole. They believed that to repent of their own sins would help bring about the salvation of their people, that spiritual progress for all was dependant on the progress of each. Whether true or not, there is no doubt this manner of thinking animated the founding of America as well—a people spiritually cleansed, who could perceive and follow the divine leading and thus bless the whole world by example—this was the animating spirit of the early settlers. Americans once commonly thought of themselves as a nation of repentant sinners, but also as a nation which welcomed divine scrutiny. Is that true today?

For each person, once the decision is made to turn toward God, the Father's searching gaze lights all the hidden places of his soul. His light cannot be blocked, nor can we steel ourselves against it, nor turn away in shame. Sins, once buried, are now revealed to full consciousness. Alchemists often spoke of the burning away of the dross from the gold, and if they spoke in metaphor, then they were talking of spiritual cleansing—a cleansing with fire—the light which brings pain.

Sins of commission, sins of omission, sins of thought, sins of word, sins of deed or no deed. All those things we should or shouldn't have done, thought or said, every past regret is lit up and revealed, exposed to our consciousness and to our spirit Father, a lifetime of mistakes brought vividly back to life. And yet we must be cleansed of this sin in our souls, or how could our souls follow the Father's good spirit back into the heavenly realms from whence he comes? Of course we cannot make ourselves worthy, anymore than we can cleanse ourselves of sin, but we can allow this painful baptism. We can allow the Father to bring those shameful memories to our minds and remind us how far we have to go.

Of man, it is required that he turn away from his bestial nature. Animals cannot do so, only man is thus endowed. So at times we must experience regret, and be filled with sorrowful remorse over our sins. We are more than flesh and bone; we are indwelt by a living spirit who gives us this choice—the choice to be more than we are—the choice to leave animal impulse and selfish desire behind. We may draw a little closer to the reality of the person our Father wants us to be—the person he created us to become.

> And my tears, make a heavenly Lethean flood,
> And drown in it my sins' black memory.
> That thou remember them, some claim as debt;

I think it mercy, if thou wilt forget.
— John Donne

    Does the Father forget our sins when we enter the next life, and in his mercy, perhaps, allow us to forget them as well? Would the good Father bring the torments of hell into our heavenly estate? This thought makes it even more imperative to experience true repentance here and now, however painful or difficult it might be. The eternal goal is worth any price.

    Gaining entrance into the heavenly kingdom cannot be effortless; for if it were, this life would be rendered meaningless. We have been created in an imperfect state with the ability to gradually become more perfect through self understanding, self-control and moral choice. The intelligent person knows what he is doing, why he is doing it, where he is going and how he will get there. In order for virtue to be cultivated, therefore, one must be able to distinguish a goal. Without that eternal goal, man is left without direction and thus, even if moral motives are cultivated for their own sake, they easily evaporate under pressure, which is something secular humanists often fail to contemplate.

    Virtue is a living experience, it is the experience of progress in attuning one's life and will with the higher mind and will of the cosmos. It is the experience of increasing internal harmony, balance and sense of proportion. One may readily observe the effect of this effort to remove man's eternal goal from the modern world—maturity is in desperately short supply. Duty cannot be perceived in the absence of moral insight and without a sense of duty, loyalty to a higher ideal, mankind quickly devolves to the level of a clever beast—all moral striving is lost. Today the basest immorality is celebrated in our ubiquitous entertainments.

    Science, in its attempt to substitute for religion, offers

nothing more than a string of proclamations exclaiming: "The end is near" These come in two varieties: "It's all your fault" (therefore you deserve to suffer) and "There is nothing you can do about it" (suffering will not atone—nothing will). Both are equally disastrous for the development of children, but it seems the best we can do is to continue to stress "scientific education" as the answer to all our ills. We are succeeding only in inculcating our young people with a messianic environmental fanaticism, or in giving them a sheer sense of hopelessness which they immediately drown out with entertainment or drugs or both. These are our future civilization builders. What manner of civilization will they build?

Nothing can replace the inborn yearning for God. And as much as men like Daniel Dennett and Richard Dawkins might wish it to be, that yearning cannot be educated away. Man needs an immovable star toward which his efforts may always be tending. Human beings will never stop needing God or stop yearning to experience the divine gaze, however painful that searching gaze may be. "Help me Father, for I have sinned," is a universal human cry.

The great question before us now is whether our nation, which once experienced complete certainty of divine favor, can now withstand the divine gaze. Have we squandered our God-given promise so soon? Is there no turning back from the precipice where we find ourselves? Someday perhaps, a new John the Baptist will rise up and say: "the way is hard, the choices are painful, but we can do no other. Our mistakes and regrets cannot and should not be forgotten here on earth. We must learn from them and accept the harsh consequences of our errors, but these will be forgotten in eternity. Repent, but also rejoice, for there is one who will show us the way. We are not lost."

- 3 -
That Ghost in the Machine

Why seek ye the living among the dead?
—Luke 24:5

LIKE MANY people, I often watch crime dramas on television to pass the evenings and I've noticed a subtle change lately as to how dead bodies are described. A few years ago, all crime dramas referred to the murder victims' remains as "the body." It was universally recognized that the body at the time of death was no longer a person; the locus of personhood had either fled or had disappeared. The person was no longer there. Nowadays, however, the detective often as not will grill the murderer with sentences like: "We know you killed Julie. Where is she? Her parents want to bring Julie home."

Now, at first this might seem like a poignant way of putting things, designed to appeal to the conscience of the fictional killer, but it is now so widespread, I am convinced that something else is afoot and that is a widespread confusion between levels of reality. These dramas seem to be affirming the claims of material reductionists that the person *is* the body and nothing more. Death simply indicates a body has been broken beyond repair, so that theoretically, when we learn to be master repairmen of our bodies, we will then never die. This, I suppose, is also the logic behind cryogenics—the body is all that exists of personhood.

I also watched a NOVA program on dreams in which Sigmund Freud was briefly mentioned only to be thrown overboard by scientists who ridiculed the very idea of mind, let alone that mind could contain levels like a subconscious. After watching an hour of mice, cats and humans all fitted out with electrodes on their heads while they dreamt, it was deduced that mice dreamt about a typical mouse day like running a maze. Cats dreamt about typical cat day of catching mice and humans were similarly rehearsing their own hypothetical futures. Evolution, you see, has equipped animals like us with the ability to practice in our dreams the problems we will encounter in our waking life.

There was no acknowledgment of the subconscious, and certainly no superconscious, only the waking and sleeping brain, which, these scientists seem to assume, is also the locus of personhood. All the complex symbolism of dream life was put down to the random firing of electrical impulses without the slightest trace of doubt. The pioneers of the study of the human mind were dismissed as so many quacks, as mind was deemed to have no reality apart from the brain. It seems that scientists, when confronted with reality that doesn't fit their material model, often simply dismiss it. Raymond Tallis, a neuroscientist himself, explains how neuroscience cannot even account for the basics of perception for it cannot explain how the gaze proceeds outward, let alone explain the personhood of the one who does the gazing.

A good place to begin understanding why consciousness is not strictly reducible to the material is

in looking at consciousness of material objects —
that is, straightforward perception. Perception as it is
experienced by human beings is the explicit sense of
being aware of something material other than oneself. Consider your awareness of a glass sitting on a
table near you. Light reflects from the glass, enters
your eyes, and triggers activity in your visual pathways. The standard neuroscientific account says that
your perception of the glass is the result of, or just
is, this neural activity. There is a chain of causes and
effects connecting the glass with the neural activity
in your brain that is entirely compatible with, as in
Dennett's words, "the same physical principles, laws,
and raw materials that suffice" to explain everything
else in the material universe.

Unfortunately for neuroscientism, the inward causal
path explains how the light gets into your brain but
not how it results in a gaze that looks out. The inward causal path does not deliver your awareness of
the glass as an item explicitly separate from you — as
over there with respect to yourself, who is over here.
This aspect of consciousness is known as intentionality (which is not to be confused with intentions).
Intentionality designates the way that we are conscious of something, and that the contents of our
consciousness are thus about something; and, in the
case of human consciousness, that we are conscious
of it as something other than ourselves. But there is
nothing in the activity of the visual cortex, consist-
ing of nerve impulses that are no more than material
events in a material object, which could make that
activity be about the things that you see. In other
words, in intentionality we have something funda-

mental about consciousness that is left unexplained
by the neurological account.[1]

Clearly, we are dealing with a situation much like the
time when the Church was confronted with facts which did
not conform to its approved model of reality and was forced
to deny those facts and to suppress them. Materialism can
never be an adequate model for the whole of reality because
it cannot account for consciousness, much less the person
who is conscious of his consciousness and who values it.

The larger question is, why should scientists continue
to insist that we look for the higher realities among the lower
and to deny the reality of mind and value? For their model
of the world to work, there would be no difference between
the dead and the living and yet they cling to that model with
brute tenaciousness, belittling all who might point out its
inadequacies as unrealistic dreamers.

Scientists continually ask us to deny the reality of our
own experience and put every human mystery down to the
"complexity" of the brain. But no matter how complex the
brain is, it could not teach us during the night season, as
sometimes occurs in normal human experience, without a
higher level of consciousness being involved. Human morality could not progress, neither individually nor collectively,
without higher values being sought as realities. Truth can
only be sought if one believes in Truth and the ability of human beings to attain ever higher and more integrated levels
of truth. Those who have not experienced ascending value
cannot claim there is no such thing anymore than one could
claim Berlin does not exist because he hasn't been there. And
the fact remains that the higher one ascends in the realm
of value, the further one can see, or rather, the deeper one

---

1 Tallis, Raymond "What Neuroscience Cannot Tell Us About Ourselves"
The New Atlantis, Fall 2010.

can see into the nature of reality. This is as true of the moral realm as it is of the physical realm.

It is true because, while the values (Truth, Beauty and Goodness) are absolute, the human pursuit of value is inherently progressive. As one pursues Goodness, one becomes more moral (personally possessing more good), and the same is true for society at large. When man rejects the reality of value, the reality of Goodness, then the pursuit of that reality ceases, and moral progress comes to an end and degeneracy begins.

It seems self evident that if you convince human beings that they are nothing more than beasts, they will very soon begin acting like beasts—snarling and fighting over scraps like wolves, tearing into each other's lives with spiteful disregard for human feeling. Selfishness reigns today because people have become convinced, due to the unceasing efforts of our Darwinian scientists over the last century, that there is nothing higher than physical pleasure or personal power for which to strive. But it seems to me, if you convince people they are nothing more than machines whose decisions are ultimately meaningless, then you create something much worse. There is no limit to the tortures machines may inflict upon other machines even if they must call upon "the greatest good for the largest number" in order to justify it.

American technology, for example, has developed tiny drones which look and fly like hummingbirds[2] and can hover near windows or perch upon windowsills in order to peer into homes, or follow their subjects around undetected, and there are unconfirmed rumors of drones being able to peer through walls entirely. Since drones are already being used on our Southern border, it will take a strong government to be able to resist the temptation of turning this technology

---

2 Watson, Julie "On the Wings of Technology: Hummingbird Drones" Associated Press, Feb. 28, 2011.

on its own citizens.[3] Unfortunately for us, America has had an almost unbroken succession of weak and divided governments with vacillating leadership since the end of the Second World War. A brave new police state will be within the grasp of our government soon and our scientific philosophers will have offered no defense, indeed have offered encouragement of it. For if we are will-less machines to begin with, in reality, we have no freedom to lose.

The majority of scientists will continue to insist that Truth can be found in matter as though the mere accumulation of facts alone could account for the integration and meaning of mind, the prioritization of value, and the persistence of personhood amid the continually changing nature of the material brain and body. This is not to suggest that science itself must be overthrown, simply that scientists have to realize their area of specialty (matter) is not the whole of reality. Philosophers and theologians are beginning to reassert their own ascendancy within their dominions and to push back the encroachment of this brand of pseudo-science. The whole of man is not found in the material mechanism of the body, and ultimately, human truth must be sought in that which is higher than mind—not lower. Once again the age old struggle between life and death, freedom and bondage is playing out. For freedom to prevail, man must begin to grasp the nature of free will, reject the ridiculously confident assertions of materialism and once again begin to marvel at the ghost within the machine.

---

3 By 2014, drones were being used by police and federal agents all across the country.

- 4 -
The Demise of the Good Father

UNTIL VERY recently, the role of father was granted great respect in our culture and the image of the good father was a source of societal integration or at least one of widespread social agreement. Mass entertainment, including movies and television, generally supported the idea that to aspire to being a good father, was something noble as well as commonplace and accessible. The father was loved, trusted and revered. The image of the good father was everywhere. On television we had *Father Knows Best*, *My Three Sons*, *Make Room For Daddy*, *Leave It To Beaver*, *Bonanza* and so on. In movies the quintessential good father was often played by Gregory Peck (*The Yearling, To Kill a Mockingbird*), but the good father was also found in Westerns (Van Heflin in *Shane*, Jimmy Stewart in *Shenandoah*). This began to change during the sixties when, in situation comedies on television, the father of the family became the butt of jokes (Archie Bunker) and this trend has continued ever since with a brief revival of the good father in the 1980s with *The Cosby Show*. All the while, the image of the bad father was becoming more commonplace (*Married with Children*) even if it was quite shocking at

31

first as in Christopher Walken's portrayal in *At Close Range.* Today, fathers, like priests, are automatically suspect. Casey Anthony was able to make an allegation of sexual abuse against her father (with no substantiating evidence) and was believed by the jury, at least to some extent, during her murder trial because suspicion of fathers is at an all time high. From Oprah Winfrey's repressed memories to Kathryn Harrison's *The Kiss* to crime dramas in which the innocent-seeming father is often revealed to be the villain, all these images combine to undermine our trust in fathers. Underneath all this is the loss of faith in the ultimate Father, God the Father, and a loss of trust in God's fatherly nature which was once taken as self-evident. God-knowing souls throughout the ages have repeatedly confirmed that God is not simply like a father, but acts consistently *as* a father, a good father, even a perfect father in the lives of the faithful.

Common religious understanding allows that the Heavenly Father bids his children to come to him and provides everything needful for us to do so in complete freedom. I think it is safe to say that coercion has no part in our understanding of the divine plan; and in fact, the existence of forced conformity in any belief system may be seen as evidence of its falsity. In truth, we are free at every stage to accept or reject the Father's leading, in all or in part, to roam away or to return. Every moral decision we make either advances or retards our progress. Human beings may indulge in acts of coercion or forcing conformity on their brethren, but the divine being never does this. The good father respects the free will of his children for the value of our love for him lies in the very freedom of its bestowal. Love is reduced to nothing if it is not freely given.

It is fashionable today to cite the very fact of our freedom as proof of God's malevolence. (And if God is malevolent, then it becomes incumbent on us to reject him.) The thinking goes that if God loved us, he would not allow the natural outworking that often results from our own free choosing—cruelty, violence, destruction and death. The fact that God allows evil to temporarily flourish, does not mean he creates evil unless our philosophy rejects the idea of free will. For in order to save us from ourselves, the Father would be forced to remove our free will which is the very purpose of our creation, the very thing which makes us valuable to him and which makes life valuable to us. The fact that God allows the temporary manifestation of evil as the natural result of human freedom, does not mean God is evil.

The question then becomes, would there be value inherent in the life of a will-less computer-minded robot whose value is found only in its function as a cog in the wheel of divine will? An example of this thinking is found in Islam where a man's value is measured by his conformity to, and function within, the Islamic system. The individual human being has no intrinsic value in himself—the individual is sacrificed to the system. In Islam, Allah may be described as a king or a judge, but he cannot be described as a father, much less a good father.

Faith is rightly defined as *trust in God*. Implicit in this is not only the idea that God is good, but that God is knowable. One cannot develop trust in an unknowable being. Faith may also be defined as having the belief in one's own ability to know God. If a person doesn't believe he can know God, he can have no relationship with God and can therefore never develop faith in God. In Islam, God is defined as thoroughly transcendent and unknowable, therefore Islam itself cannot properly be defined as a "faith" in the Western sense of the word.

Faith is the knowledge that God is a father who is properly trusted by his children to lead them from darkness to light, from unknowing animal fear to the peace and security which comes with accepting divine love and trusting in the Father's goodness, and trusting that his truth, beauty and goodness may be known through experience. Speaking of faith, reason and the Islamic position that God is unknowable, Pope Benedict XVI said:

> In all honesty, one must observe that in the late Middle Ages we find trends in theology which would sunder this synthesis between the Greek spirit and the Christian spirit. In contrast with the so-called intellectualism of Augustine and Thomas, there arose with Duns Scotus a voluntarism which, in its later developments, led to the claim that we can only know God's *voluntas ordinata*. Beyond this is the realm of God's freedom, in virtue of which he could have done the opposite of everything he has actually done. This gives rise to positions which clearly approach those of Ibn Hazn and might even lead to the image of a capricious God, who is not even bound to truth and goodness. God's transcendence and otherness are so exalted that our reason, our sense of the true and good, are no longer an authentic mirror of God, whose deepest possibilities remain eternally unattainable and hidden behind his actual decisions. As opposed to this, the faith of the Church has always insisted that between God and us, between his eternal Creator Spirit and our created reason there exists a real analogy, in which—as the Fourth Lateran Council in 1215 stated—unlikeness remains infinitely greater than likeness, yet not to the point of abolishing analogy and its language. God does not become more divine when we push him away from us in a sheer, impenetrable voluntarism; rather, the truly divine God is the God who has revealed him-

self as *logos* and, as *logos*, has acted and continues to act lovingly on our behalf. Certainly, love, as Saint Paul says, "transcends" knowledge and is thereby capable of perceiving more than thought alone (cf. Eph 3:19); nonetheless it continues to be love of the God who is *Logos*. Consequently, Christian worship is, again to quote Paul, "worship in harmony with the eternal Word and with our reason. (cf. Rom 12:1).[1]

By constructing an impenetrable wall between man and God, Islam does not increase the divinity of God, but rather dissevers God from his nature (as absolute Truth, Beauty and Goodness) and from the reality of man's experience of God, thus enabling the substitution of the dead law of Islam for the individual experience of God's love and the individual discovery of his will as greater than his own.

The image of the good father has all but disappeared in the modern world. With what, then, will it be replaced?

---

1 Pope Benedict XVI Speech at the University of Regensburg Germany, September 12, 2006.

- 5 -
The Embarrassment of Morality

THERE ONCE WAS a time, not so very long ago, when Americans felt the need to express a moral viewpoint or to reach for the moral level in art, literature, popular entertainment and politics. Watching old movies or television shows from fifty years ago, one is immediately struck by the moral tone which then prevailed even when, or especially when, these stories depicted immoral acts. In the 1950's parents felt perfectly safe leaving their children to watch the "Andy Griffith Show" or "Gunsmoke" or pretty much anything else on television. We didn't need specialized children's programming then. We were united by our values. But perhaps by the time Thornton Wilder wrote *Our Town*, America was already passing out of what my 99 year-old friend called "a simpler time." I think what she meant by that was a shared moral culture marked by simple moral striving: a time when self-respect was more important than material gain and "how the game was played" much more important than mere winning. These ideas seem quaint now, when business is marked by ruthless cunning and material accumulation is counted as the singular measure of success. Everyone gets away with what he can and those who stubbornly cling to moral behavior are thought of as naïve or old fashioned. We've become the worst sort of cynics, expecting the worst of our fellows. Moral concern has become slightly embarrassing while absolute moral disregard is not.

Our politicians no longer feel obliged to add a moral dimension to their arguments the way they once did, even on the gravest subjects of war and peace. Think of the Lincoln-Douglas debates and how each side quoted easily and readily from scripture in order to illustrate the indispensible moral dimension of their cause. Today, it is very difficult to find a political argument that goes beyond bare utility. Of course, one still hears appeals to compassion for the less fortunate and the like, but the age when the making of a moral argument in the political sphere was required appears to be quite past.

Of course, politicians are not above using the power of church organizations to help boost their bids for election, but they are not about to be used by religion, to see themselves as an instrument of God's will, or to give up any element of personal prerogative as a sacrifice for a higher truth in the way George Washington or Abraham Lincoln did. We have a plethora of candidates with many good ideas they would like to implement, but few with high ideals they would like to live up to.

Pastor Terry Jones, perhaps, was such a person (almost on the order of John Brown, forcing the country to face unpleasant realities) and he has been universally derided as either a fanatic or a clown. Senate majority leader Harry Reid recently omitted the words "under God" from his recitation of the Pledge of Allegiance. And though most, if not all, of our holders of high public office would readily affirm their own "firmness in the right," few, if any, would qualify that statement as Lincoln did, with "as God gives us to see the right." The idea that perhaps we cannot always apprehend "the right" through our own intellectual power is anathema to modern man—an affront to the sovereignty of his will and a curtailment of what he perceives as his freedom.

Orators and politicians of the past could rely on a shared moral and cultural vision of reality, a deep well of shared cultural experience from which they could draw understanding and support. Politicians seldom quote from the bible now. First, they cannot rely on their audience to be familiar enough with scripture to understand the allusion and secondly, they can count on a press generally hostile to religion to spin it as preachy, condescending or "out of touch."

Bill Clinton demonstrated how a high intelligence coupled with low, or rather average, morality does not make for a strong President. The country then swung the other way in electing George W. Bush, a man perceived as having average intelligence but a higher moral character (higher than that of Bill Clinton, at any rate). Practically the entire argument for the election of George W. Bush was based upon character and the country bought the idea that both he and his wife, Laura, were "good, decent people" who embodied a kind of "Mr. Smith goes to Washington" ideal. No challenge could be so difficult that strong American morality and idealism could not cope. Unfortunately, this reliance on character (or rather, the image of character) masked a decided lack of intellectual curiosity and inability to imagine the motivation of human beings whose world views are entirely different from his own. As Mrs. Bush wrote in her memoir, "Not only can't I empathize with the mother of a suicide bomber, I can't even imagine her."[1] Neither George Bush, nor his family, nor his

---

1 Bush, Laura, *Spoken from the Heart* (New York: Scribner, 2010) pg. 286.

advisers, apparently, could imaginatively place themselves into minds shaped and conditioned by Islam. That would have taken a lot of reading (burning the midnight oil) and George Bush was no John Quincy Adams.

Lack of imagination was not the only problem. The following paragraph written by Laura Bush illustrates the sloppy thinking and overreliance on simplistic American notions of right and wrong that marred the Iraq operation:

> In World War II, we knew that if we crippled the enemy in one place, other fronts would weaken and eventually collapse. During the Cold War, the United States could cede some countries, such as Cuba or Eastern Europe or Vietnam, or even Afghanistan up until 1979, to the Soviet's sphere and still the fundamental balance of power would remain unchanged. Yet in this new type of war, against not an army in uniform, but a radical ideology [*the "radical ideology" is undefined*] bent on destroying the very framework of our shared civilization, we could not write off one country to the enemy. [*The "enemy" is undefined, therefore the countries already "written off" are undefined. This blindness continues to prevent us from acknowledging the Organization of Islamic Conference as the hostile bloc it is.*] Never before in history had such small numbers possessed the potential to inflict such horrific damage. [*They are small in number only if we choose to disregard all those they represent.*] So wherever the terrorists were plotting destruction, we had to engage them. [*Notice "the enemy" has morphed into the even more generic "terrorists."*] And wherever terrorist cells might be trying to gain a foothold, we had to turn them back. [*There have been "terrorist cells" in*

Britain, Europe and our own country for decades now and I know of little that has been done to "turn them back."] It was a war of terrorist acts and a contest of ideology, and we could not win unless we met them firmly on every front. We could not let Iraq fail, or let the United States fail in Iraq. [*Again we see the poor definition of words. Throughout the Bush administration, officials seemed to equate withdrawal with "failure" and therefore success becomes defined simply as the dogged entrenchment of our troops in that dreadful country.*] We could never again allow a full-fledged haven for terror to flourish if we wanted to protect Americans inside the borders of our own nation. [*Mrs. Bush might have been forgiven for spouting this rhetoric in 2001, but her book was written in 2010, long after it became fully apparent that "terrorist havens" may be found wherever there are sufficient numbers of Muslims. Britain has turned out to be one of the chief exporters of terror. The 9-11 plot was actually hatched in Hamburg. What are we going to do about that?*] Nor could we give up on the millions of Iraqis who were hoping that the extremists would be turned back and a free society would have a chance to take hold. [*Were there really "millions" of Iraqis hoping for a "free society?" How do they define "free society?" How does Mrs. Bush know what those millions really want?*] George chose the best way he thought to win, and we waited. And we prayed for the men and women who had pledged to fight for our country and for our freedoms.[2]

Eleven years of struggle with Iraq, and we are still waiting for the glorious outcome once promised: Iraq

---

2 *Ibid.*, pg. 384.

would become our stable, unified and democratic ally and show their gratitude for liberation by granting generous oil concessions and purchasing our weaponry. At what point will we realize that we cannot remake the Muslim world in our image? At what point should we insist Muslim peoples and polities face the consequences of their own making, consequences, incidentally, from which they have no desire to be rescued?

A more realistic strategy is to allow our Sunni and Shi'a enemies to war with each other while providing support for an ethnic enclave (Kurdistan) on the condition they provide sanctuary for other ethnic and religious minorities.

The larger problem, however, is the reluctance to confront Islam on moral ground which is its weakest point. The solid moral language of the past has evaporated along with any pretense of moral leadership. But cast the light of *any* other religion on Islam and it is shown as the false and destructive ideology it is. Spiritual peace and comfort are foreign to Islam. It produces pride, belligerence and disquiet among its adherents—keeping grown men in a perpetual state of frustrated adolescence. It lacks an overriding moral structure and the only "good" it recognizes is the physical triumph of Islam. It is only proper that we should look to other religions, actual religions, for guidance and inspiration. We have a rich spiritual heritage on which to draw. For example:

> **Buddhism:** Those who imagine evil where there is none, and do not see evil where it is—upholding false views, they go to states of woe. Those who discern the wrong as wrong and the right as right—upholding right views, they go to realms of bliss. (Dhammapada XXII: 318-19)

Hinduism: Man is made by his belief. As he believes, so he becomes. (Bhagavad Gita)

Taoism: True goodness is like water in that it blesses everything and harms nothing. And like water, true goodness seeks the lowest places, even those levels which others avoid, and that is because it is akin to the Tao. (Tao Te Ching 81)

Judaism: Whoever sows injustice reaps calamity (Proverbs 22:8); they who sow the wind shall reap the whirlwind. (Hosea 8:7)

Christianity: Beware of false prophets, which come to you in sheep's clothing, but inwardly they are ravening wolves. Ye shall know them by their fruits. Do men gather grapes of thorns, or figs of thistles? Even so every good tree bringeth forth good fruit; but a corrupt tree bringeth forth evil fruit. A good tree cannot bring forth evil fruit, neither can a corrupt tree bring forth good fruit. Every tree that bringeth not forth good fruit is hewn down, and cast into the fire. Wherefore by their fruits ye shall know them. (Matthew 7: 15-20)

What would be easier than to delve into our rich heritage of true religion and allow it to define itself and thus to show Islam to be wholly outside? Are not all true religions the province of value—of goodness, truth and beauty—and chiefly concerned with the correct apprehending of value so as to lead men to pursue it and thus, to mature? We need to regain our religious vocabulary: one that is sure and steady, but which need not begin and end with

Christianity. We cannot shrink from confronting immorality especially when it comes to us in the false form of religion. In the words of Lao Tse, "Knowing ignorance is strength. Ignoring knowledge is sickness."

- 6 -
Why Islam is Not a Religion

WHAT FOLLOWS is a summary of the arguments presented in my previous book, *Allah is Dead: Why Islam is Not a Religion*. In our ongoing discussion of what religion actually is, it is also important to discuss what it is not, or at least, what it should not be.

Many people in our post-Christian society (especially journalists) are afraid of religion, misinformed about it and ignorant of the most basic theological terms and concepts. And our theologians are often too specialized in their work to be able to discuss religion in its broadest outlines and our Churchmen are often so concerned with finding common ground that they gloss over and ignore the theology of Islam.

Our greatest Islam critics confine their attack to the non-religious aspects of Islam, either its political side or its judicial side. But when we discuss political Islam or Sharia law alone, we imply that there is a religious Islam that is perfectly fine, that we don't have to worry about. And we leave the major problems of Islamization—Muslim immigration, mosque building, the proselytizing in our prisons and military and the infiltration of our governmental institutions completely untouched and indeed untouchable.

We need to take a few steps back to examine Islam as a

whole and to broadly define the outlines of Islam—what it is and what it isn't.

One thing we can definitely say about Islam is that it is not solely confined to a belief system. If it is a religion it is not a religion only. Islam is a total system of life and contains within itself a particular social system, judicial system, and political system which includes geo-political aspirations— the conquest and administration of territory.

I often liken Islam to a duck-billed platypus which su- perficially resembles an otter. Upon closer examination, one finds this animal has a duck-like bill, lays eggs, and has many other characteristics which are not otter-like at all. Therefore, it cannot remain in the biological category containing otters. It is simply too different and requires its own category. I believe the same thing is true of Islam. It is much too differ- ent from the other religions to remain in the religion-only category, it should be uniquely classified in its own category.

Secondly, I think it is obvious to Christians that Is- lam is its polar opposite and I believe nihilism lies between Christianity and Islam and that the morality of Islam is in- verted.

CHRISTIANITY	NIHILISM	ISLAM
Spirit (Morality)		Matter
Loving God	No God	Malevolent God
Benevelant Universe	Indifferent Universe	Preditory Universe
	No morality	
Matter		Spirit (Moralty)

Let me explain: religion supplies our basic world-view concerning the nature of reality. If we were to plot belief sys- tems on a graph—on one side are religions which view God as good and the universe as a benevolent place—in the middle we have the view that there is no God and the universe is a pitiless and indifferent place, the view of material determinism, which is the direction toward which our society is tending. On the other side is the view of God as malevolent and the universe is a vicious and unpredictable place—that God enjoys our suffering. This is where Islam lies.

The reason we can assert that the morality of Islam is inverted is that Islam consistently elevates material over spiritual considerations. That is, it elevates the material obedience to the dictates of the Islamic doctrine above all consideration of Truth or Goodness. Morality, conformity and even legality are all one and the same in Islam. Let me give you an example: The following are the words of the father of a failed female suicide bomber:

> "'If I had known what [my daughter] was planning I would have told the Jews. I would have stopped her."

> "In our religion it is forbidden for a girl's body to be uncovered even at home. How could a girl allow her body to be smashed to pieces and then collected up by Jews? This is absolutely forbidden."[1]

Though this is an extreme circumstance, we see this pattern play out over and over again. Women are treated as if they were property because that is how they are defined by Islam.

For example, if a young girl runs away from home to marry her true love, she has in effect stolen the property, that is herself, from her family and the family will often try

---

1 Toolis, Kevin "Face to face with the women suicide bombers" *The Daily Mail* Feb. 7, 2009.

to kill her to negate the theft and to assuage the shame and humiliation suffered by the family for not being in full control of their daughter's body as is required by Islam. In this way, Islam is utterly materialistic—control of the body is everything. And the Muslim mind is fully focused on the material world.

I further contend that Islam has become a substitute God for Muslims. Worship is defined as obedience to Islam and Islam represents the entire will of God for all men through all time. God's will is also every single thing that happens. So even if one disobeys Islam, it is still God's will that he did so.

If there is no difference between man's will and God's will, there is no God to seek. In Islam God is unknowable—he is completely transcendent and his will is all things. Theologically this is the equivalent to saying there is no God.

Furthermore, when a religion becomes completely reduced to a doctrine and only a doctrine, it is no longer a living faith. It is dead. Islam may be complex and it may be logical, but it is logic in the absence of living truth.

Religion in its broadest sense must be about the pursuit of higher value—of Truth, Beauty and Goodness. As we learned in philosophy class, the thinking used to be that these values stand apart from the world and evaluate the world. Truth is the measure of man, man is not the measure of truth. That is the essence of religious thought. And the interesting thing is that when we pursue value, as all true religions encourage, we incorporate those values into our selves—as we pursue goodness, we become good, as we pursue truth we reflect truth in ourselves and we appreciate the beauty of God's creation more and more. This is commonly called spiritual growth. All religion, as we have known it, facilitates this process: its goal is to lead men to God and lead them to experience God's love.

Islam on the other hand, subordinates everything to itself. Islam is the highest value and the spiritual values we just mentioned are thought to be entirely contained within Islam, even to be entirely contained within the Koran. Which is why after a rumor was started by *Newsweek* about Korans being flushed down the toilet at Guantanamo in May 2005, scores were killed and hundreds injured in rioting all over the Muslim world. Lives were sacrificed over paper and ink. We saw the same pattern play out with the Muhammad cartoons over a supposed religious principle which concerns only the material world.

There is no higher truth than Islam, no higher good than Islam and nothing more beautiful than Islam. Islam has replaced God, you see, and its ultimate goal is not to lead men to seek those higher values. Islam exists simply to perpetuate itself.

Let us take three simple religious concepts and look at how they are subordinated under Islam.

The first one is faith. When we use the word faith, we mean a growing trust in a loving, fatherly God—a God who can be known, a God who can be approached. In Islam, God cannot be known, there is no bridge to him. What Muslims mean by faith is faith in the truth and rightness of Islam itself. Intellectual assent to a doctrine has replaced living faith which is man's relationship with a higher reality.

The second is prayer. When we pray we open our inner life to God—it is an intimate and personal communication and is often a petition for God to strengthen us in virtue so we will be better prepared to meet the problems of our lives.

There is nothing personal or intimate about Muslim prayer. It is communal and a rote formula. Everyone prays the same prayers at the same time facing the same direction, while performing the same muscular movements. Just like military drills, these so-called prayers have the effect of cementing communal solidarity, but not of increasing intimate contact with God. Personal petitions must be addressed correctly to one of the 99 names of God, otherwise the prayer will be lost, as though God were some kind of giant post office. There is no intimacy between man and God in Islamic prayer because there cannot be.

The third is worship by which we mean love, adoration, awe and gratitude all being expressed to God. Often this is done in the form of song. In Islam, worship is defined as obedience to Islam and since God is transcendent and we cannot know him, loving him is beside the point and is certainly not essential. Obedience is everything.

This concept is also a major stumbling block to democracy because to obey man's law in Islamic thought is equivalent to the worship of man. Now, while I would agree that the worship of man is broadly a characteristic of the modern world, especially if we look at the rise of science and its promise of omniscience and even omnipotence—that all things can be known and done through the agency of science. I vehemently disagree that the Islamic total belief system and total regulation of life is the answer to anything. It is certainly not a way to grow closer to God. It leads men away from God and focuses the mind on the material world alone from morning till night, day in and day out.

Islam is not the answer—Islam is the problem.

Now for those who still insist that Islam remain in the religion category, they will eventually have to concede that Islam is either a false religion or an evil religion because it leads men to evil action, even toward their own families. Of course there is no rule stating all religions must be good or lead to good actions.

Islam is false because it is built on the fundamental lie that Muhammad was a real prophet, rather than a man simply pretending to be a prophet in order to gain power over people, or a myth altogether. Of course one can make the same claim about Joseph Smith or L. Ron Hubbard or any number of other founders of man-made religions which have been created from time to time throughout history. A religion which venerates an evil man and raises him to the level of the perfect model for human conduct, cannot help but lead men to evil action – even *jihad*.

This brings us back to the crux of our problem. Should an evil religion, which functions in exactly the opposite way from religion as we have known it, receive the same benefits and consideration as religion which is beneficial to society?

Essentially our secular society has a contract with religion. It says, the state will not interfere with religious practice so long as it is within the law and the state will extend benefits in the form of tax breaks and other considerations so that religious institutions can flourish freely within our borders. In exchange, religion has strengthened the family, produced honest, hard-working citizens with a high degree of personal self-control so that people behave ethically and charitably toward each other and can function with a minimum of external social control.

Religion as we have known it has been good for society. It has nurtured morality, strengthened the family, fostered public service and encouraged social harmony. Islam, on the other hand, is self-segregating and fosters ideas of Muslim supremacy. It thereby sows seeds of social discord. Even its tradition of charitable giving is solely for the benefit of fellow Muslims and it utterly destroys the nuclear family through its adoption of polygamy. Polygamous marriage is not marriage. It reduces women to the status of property. Even Mormon polygamy eventually does this.

With the Arab Spring we can clearly see that when the governing police state is suddenly removed, Muslim societies across the board descend into violence and chaos—religious sects fight other sects, tribes fight other tribes, looting is rampant and men are reduced to defending their families against their neighbors. Needless to say, this is not what we expect from religion. We expect religion to uphold morality and civilizational standards. It is clear Islam does not do so.

Now despite all the evidence that Islam is an immoral religion, there is a current of modern thought seeking to elevate a laudable personal virtue, that of tolerance, over the greater social principle of justice.

But is it just to tolerate polygamy in the name of religious freedom? The Supreme Court unanimously ruled in 1878 that it is not. Is it just to tolerate the unequal right to inheritance for women? Is it just to tolerate forced marriage? Is it just to tolerate antisemitism? Is it just to tolerate the preaching of hatred toward non-Muslims? Is it just to tolerate the teaching that Muslims are superior to non-Muslims or that men are superior to women? Is it just to tolerate a parallel legal system based on inequality?

There are things that our society cannot tolerate and expect to survive. Justice must take its rightful place above tolerance.

So to reiterate once more, Islam is not a religion because:

It is an amalgam of social, political and judicial systems as well as a belief system. It is neither one thing nor the other—Islam is unique.

Philosophically it is as far from other religions as it is possible to be. It lies beyond nihilism and its morality is inverted.

In society, Islam functions in the opposite manner

from all other religions. Rather than producing peace and social harmony, it sows violence and social disruption.

Therefore, I believe it would be wise to reconsider Islam's inclusion as a religion at least as far as the First Amendment is concerned. I understand the difficulties with this approach, and I know many have and will reject it, but I also think it is necessary to raise the question about what Islam really is and what it isn't.

When you consider the effort that went into arguing whether Pluto should be considered a planet or not, or how a newly discovered insect should be classified, or what constitutes organic produce, I really don't think the ability to classify belief systems is beyond us. At the very least we must call into question this Islam-is-a-religion trump card that its defenders have been playing so successfully. And I think it could help remove the confusion in our own ranks and allow Islam to be criticized in its entirety, not just as a political or judicial system.

We cannot fight a lie of this magnitude with half the truth.

- 7 -
Religion and the Law

ACCORDING TO the Internal Revenue Manual 7(10)69, Exempt Organizations Examination Guidelines Handbook, text 321.3(3), an organization is defined as a "church" if it has the following broadly and neutrally defined characteristics: (a) a distinct legal existence, (b) a recognized creed and form of worship, (c) a definite and distinct ecclesiastical government, (d) a formal code of doctrine and discipline, (e) a distinct religious history, (f) a membership not associated with any other church or denomination, (g) an organization of ordained ministers, (h) ordained ministers selected after completing prescribed studies, (i) a literature of its own, (j) established places of worship, (k) regular congregations, (l) regular religious services, (m) Sunday schools for religious instruction of the young, (n) schools for the preparation of its ministers, and (o) any other facts and circumstances that may bear upon the organization's claim for church status.

Though this definition was developed in a purely Christian context for the purpose of determining tax-exempt status for various newly-formed sects, it is clear that Satanists who sacrifice kittens could gain status as a "church" so long as they conduct their sacrifices according to their own formal code at a regular place and time, with their own "ministers" and instruct the young in the proper manner of sacrifice according to their own literature. Just check the boxes above and you too can start a new, legal and possibly profitable tax-exempt "religion." (See for example, Scientology.)

So, how should religion be defined? In the *U.S. v. Ballard*, 322 U.S. 78 (1943), the Supreme Court stated:

> The Fathers of the Constitution were not unaware of the varied and extreme views of religious sects, of the violence of disagreement among them, and of the lack of any one religious creed on which all men would agree. They fashioned a charter of government which envisaged the widest possible toleration of conflicting views....The religious views espoused by respondents might seem incredible, if not preposterous, to most people. But if those doctrines are subject to trial before a jury charged with finding their truth or falsity, then the same can be done with the religious beliefs of any sect. When the triers of fact undertake that task, they enter a forbidden domain.

This seems to imply not only that religion should not be properly defined for legal purposes, but that religion cannot be so defined. And certainly the very thought of wading into the religious realm is anathema to most legal minds.

Implicit in this assessment is the idea that religion need have no relation to truth. Religion can be entirely a matter of falsehood and delusion and still be considered a "true" religion so long as the boxes above are ticked. Though wrapped in the cloth of high-mindedness, this seems to me a cowardly abandonment of judicial responsibility.

For many years I have maintained that Islam, because of its many disparate features (including complete and self-contained political and judicial systems) should not be properly or legally categorized as a true religion.

Religion is more than a belief system which points toward a random god or gods. For religion to be actual, it must include the living spiritual experience and growing realization of love, truth, beauty and goodness—of God. God must be loved, and through that love, he must then be known. There is no other way for religion to be real in the lives of men. An abstract god who is primarily feared can never become a part of the believer's experiential reality. Fear is the experience of beasts; it is primal, never transcendent. Fear cannot bestow insight.

True religion grants insight into the nature of reality though the transcendent experience of spirit and spiritual value—which are real. True religion does not confer delusion nor foster fanaticism. It is the calm assurance that men are endowed with a living spirit and that this good spirit reveals in the light of truth, what ought to be, not simply what is. Religious insight is not a matter of logical proof, but rather what is spiritually felt to be true, bypassing mind altogether. Religious insight is a different way of knowing; it is a method of perceiving higher reality—transcendent Love—which is the essence of all things.

The logical mind can sort reality by creating categories in abstraction. Philosophy may give meaning to reality by finding relation between these categories, but only spiritual insight can elevate things and meanings by conferring value—which again, is spiritually felt. It is the growth of spiritual feeling which allows the comprehension of value, and again, value is not comprehended simply by the mind, but by the soul. The value of our country is not its GDP.

I believe it is obvious our Founding Fathers did not

intend the First Amendment's protection for freedom of religion to shelter a parallel and belligerent social, political and judicial system within our borders. They would instantly comprehend the necessity to define religion within certain boundaries for First Amendment purposes. A minority religion which encourages hatred, intolerance and violence against the majority at the very least requires containment and monitoring and cannot be allowed to spread unrestricted without ultimately threatening the nation.

Defining true religion for First Amendment protection could be easily done in neutral language and religions and religious sects could be subject to a simple test such as the following:

1) Is love, the progressive experience of God, encouraged?

2) Are the fruits of the spirit, (truthfulness, joy, peace, loyalty, long-suffering, gentleness, goodness, faith, meekness, and temperance) encouraged?

3) Is loving service to humanity, without prejudice, encouraged?

4) Are hatred, selfishness, intolerance, intemperance, disloyalty, deceit and violence discouraged?

5) Is violent coercion employed?

Thus, the court would not be required to prove or disprove the validity of any set of religious beliefs (as the justices worried about in *Ballard*) but it can set standards on what true religion should do for mankind and judge the fitness of different religions to come under the protection of the

First Amendment on that basis. Good men must not shrink from discussing religion for fear of causing offense. The time has come to robustly and honestly discuss and define the real nature of religion. All Americans must certainly admit the necessity of allowing only those religions (both new and old traditions) which are beneficial to our society to grow and flourish on our soil. Those harmful to our social unity should not be given free rein to grow in influence and power, for the day of reckoning will surely come.

A house divided against itself cannot stand.[1] Once again, we find we must struggle for union.

---

1 Matthew 12:25, quoted by Abraham Lincoln on June 16, 1858.

- 8 -
Faith, Reason and a Call to Spiritual Arms

I N AN ARTICLE entitled "Defend Christendom" published in *National Review*, Conrad Black wrote:

> Our secular leaders, whatever their own religious views, should cease to appease these forces of the anti-Christ; should unsheathe the great moral sword in their scabbards, and have some thought for the more than 1.5 billion practicing Christians whose votes they seek, while pretending that any acknowledgment of Christianity is an affront to all other faiths and a forced march on seven-league boots back into the Dark Ages.

The only problem I see with the statement is that secularity in and of itself has no moral sword which to unsheathe and therefore secular leaders are very unlikely to fully engage in moral battle, especially one involving opposition to what is supposed to be a religion, namely the system of Islam. They must have the moral guidance of true religion as well as the guidance of reason and common sense. They can act in concert with the churches but they cannot act for the churches. Our churches have a role to play that cannot be replicated by any other institution.

To the balanced personality, reason can never be imprisoned by religion, neither should reason seek to drive religion out of mind or from the public square. Faith and reason act together as two eyes to give us depth perception into the nature of reality and the nature of God. Faith and reason need each other.

It was Jesus who made the last great advancement in morality and it was he who brought us a sword with which to do moral battle—his word.[1] Therefore, it is by and through him that this battle will ultimately be fought. The only institutions suited to such a task are the churches, not political parties or nation states. For once in our lifetimes, the churches might lead and secular leaders may follow.

If the churches are to uphold their mandate and represent Christ to the world, then the churches must speak for him, not simply attempt to plead his case by engaging in endless dialogue with various Muslims who claim to represent Islam, but who actually have no real power to do so. The Pope may speak for all Catholics, but there is no one who can legitimately do the same for all Sunnis, Shi'a, Sufis, Ahmadis or other Muslim sects. Dialogue between religious leaders avails us nothing. The churches should speak directly to ordinary Muslims, bypassing their leaders altogether, just as Jesus would do.

Christ, as he looks upon the earth today, sees before him a billion or more human beings who are enslaved to a belief system shrouded in spiritual darkness. In his life, Jesus quoted Isaiah in the synagogue[2]: "The Spirit of the Lord God

---

1 See Matthew 10:34.
2 See Luke 4: 15-21.

is upon me; because the Lord hath anointed me to preach good tidings unto the meek; he hath sent me to bind up the brokenhearted, to proclaim liberty to the captives, and the opening of the prison to them that are bound."[3]

Islam is nothing less that a great spiritual prison. Its devotees see themselves as slaves of Allah and most emphatically *not* as sons of God. The only relationship Muslims may envision between themselves and Allah is one of blind obedience: absolute mental and spiritual slavery. Reason may not be employed to question Islamic doctrine, for Allah is not bound by his own laws, by his own nature, or by reason at all. Christianity, on the other hand, views reason as a way of approaching God.

Since the mid 9th Century, Islam has expressly denied that there is any "real analogy"[4] between man and God (man is not created in God's image) and therefore human reason has no basis by which to question Islam. Reason is simply irrelevant. On what possible basis, then, can real dialogue be engaged between representatives of the Hellenized Gospel and Islam? Muslims maintain Allah is pure Will, he is not Truth. God, as revealed by Jesus, is Truth and Goodness and Beauty. He is Love. His relationship with man is that of a Father. To Muslims this is pure blasphemy—Allah has no "associates" and men are not his children, but are either slaves (Muslims) or rebel enemies (non-Muslims).

Jesus charged the Apostles to go out into the world and proclaim the good news: that God is our Father who loves us and suffers none of us to perish if we turn to him. If the churches are to follow Christ, they must boldly call the mass of Muslims who now sit in spiritual darkness to the light of truth. Why shouldn't the churches empower Mus-

---

3 Isaiah 61: 1-3.

4 See Pope Benedict XVI's Regensburg address on Sept. 12, 2006 quoted in Chapter 4, "The Demise of the Good Father" on page 34.

lims to proclaim that coercing belief is not reasonable and that violence is not right? Why should churches go along with the program that deprives Muslims of the right to question Islam? The churches must respect Muslims, not Islam: churches should actively give ordinary Muslims the power to choose.

It should be possible for churches to join together to broadcast the good news into Muslim lands the way Voice of America broadcast the truth about the West into the Soviet bloc. "Neither do men light a candle, and put it under a bushel, but on a candlestick; and it giveth light unto all that are in the house."[5] The secular state cannot do this. Only the churches can do this. A program involving television, radio and the internet broadcasting the words of Christ 24 hours a day every day of the year in all the languages of the Muslim world can and should be undertaken by the churches if they are to truly follow Christ and give his word to all nations and peoples.

The first objection to such a proposal will be that Muslims will retaliate against Christians in Muslim lands, that is, the tempo of harassment, expulsion and murder of Christians will increase, so that the Muslim world will be Christian-free in five years rather than fifty. This is a very real possibility and so must be met by the churches collectively calling on our secular government to take back full control of our refugee programs and place Christians from Muslim countries at the top of the list of priorities for refugee status and Muslims from Muslim lands at the bottom. As things stand now, this priority seems to be reversed and control of our refugee program lies ultimately in the hands of the United Nations, not the people of the United States. This must be remedied by Congress.

5 Matthew 5:15.

Indeed, the churches themselves must reach out to save the bodies of our fellow Christians, but more importantly, their primary duty is to reach out to the souls of *all* our fellow human beings. They should actively deliver the good news we take for granted, but which is essentially unknown in the Muslim world. Muslims think they know what religion is, but they are only given the Islamic system. They think they know who Jesus was, but they are given Isa of the Qur'an, not the real Jesus of Nazareth who spoke words of comfort and gave hope to the world. Those who live by the sword shall die by the sword, but those who accept the words of Jesus, shall achieve life everlasting. The churches must join the great spiritual struggle for the souls of men, not sit on the sidelines in complacency, aloof from this battle of the ages.

> Faith is born of the soul, not the body. Whoever would lead someone to faith needs the ability to speak well and to reason properly, without violence and threats... To convince a reasonable soul, one does not need a strong arm, or weapons of any kind, or any other means of threatening a person with death.[6]

Jesus said, "Think not that I am come to send peace on earth: I came not to send peace, but a sword."[7] His sword is Truth—a truth that is joined to the arm of man's reason— the truth that between God and man there is a "real analogy" so that man may apprehend the living God. Let this sword cut through the lies and distortions of Islam and reveal to Muslims the living reality of God's love. God does not desire

---

6 Byzantine emperor Manuel II Paleologus to an educated Persian on the subject of Christianity and Islam quoted by Pope Benedict XVI in his Regensburg address delivered 09-12-2006 and taken from Controversy VII, 3 b–c: Khoury, pp. 144-145; Förstel vol. I, VII. Dialog 1.6, pp. 240-243.

7 See Matthew 10:34.

his children be coerced into believing in him, or coerced into obeying a rigid and unchanging dogma entirely unfit for the modern world. Spreading faith by the sword could never reasonably be taken as God's will. This truth must be proclaimed from the mountaintops, allowing Muslims to make a real and lasting choice.

- 9 -
Religion and Inspiration

I T OFTEN SEEMS there are two types of religious leaders in the world: those who desire their disciples to emulate their every thought and deed as life's greatest ideal, and those who desire to inspire others to find God in their own way by giving them guidance, but not orders. Those who aspire to be the model for righteous conduct for all time doom their latter day followers to copy customs of another time and place, making them a curiosity (as in the case of the Amish or Fundamentalist Mormons) or a serious threat to human progress (as in the case of Muslims). Sadly, they must live within their own closed systems to which the wider world is ever a threat and never a challenge.

Jesus demonstrated how it is possible for man to find God and to gradually become like God, even to become one with him, and to do so within the bounds of this short earthly life. He gave inspiration to men and women all down through the ages who desire to know God and grow in understanding of him. Never did he lay down a specific method, or decree that all who would follow him must re-enact his life's forms to the letter. Rather did he show how the divine spark might enter a man's heart and develop within and how consciousness of God can grow to such a degree that a man's every thought may eventually reflect the divine will.

Many human beings, however, want to be told exactly what to do in order to gain divine favor. I have seen people asking gurus what they should eat, when to go to bed, when to get up in the morning, what to wear and even how often they should have sex. Many people are distressed at having too much freedom and when given the choice, opt for security. These are natural human tendencies which unscrupulous religious leaders have always exploited.

There is also an unfortunate tendency among conservative circles to avoid the use of the word "spiritual" as if it were the plague. And yet all religion concerns spiritual realities and religion's primary duty is toward the human soul. (And the soul, being a spiritual reality itself, has likewise been banished from polite conversation.) Religion which concerns itself primarily with the mind, with constructing an ever more complex theological edifice, contains a very narrow appeal and is destined to divide men, not to unite them. On the other hand, religion which concerns itself primarily with good works and ministry to the body, fails in its duty to feed the soul and so fails to attract (or to hold) those seekers who hunger after righteousness and thirst for the living water of truth.

We live in an age of great spiritual blindness. A time when truth is relegated to a position of relativity and the eternal and infinite are exiled from our thoughts altogether.

The question is this: Does the living spirit of God live within the mind of man or not?

If God's spirit lives within man, then his voice is continually speaking and speaks to each generation, even if only a scant few ever hear it. God did not cease speaking after Moses, Isaiah, Jeremiah or Jesus ceased their utterances. He speaks continually to the heart of every believer even if we seldom hear, or feel, the divine voice or impression. The word is not dead letters on a page, the word is alive, and is indeed the bread of life.

True religion is dynamic and liberating. The soul is a living, ever changing, ever growing entity that requires freedom to develop its own originality. Each unique human personality self-realizes in its own way and anyone who says there is only one way to achieve immortality of the soul is certainly in error. The goal (the realization of the fatherhood of God and the consequent brotherhood of man) is unifying in itself—how each person comes to this realization is precious and unique in the universe. No man may say, "I know the complete and final truth," but each man may find his own portion of truth. This truth will lead to ever greater truth, but no two people will find it in exactly the same way.

If this is accurate, then shame on those teachers who would drag their charges back centuries and leave them in a world that no longer exists among thoughts that no longer pertain to man's present condition. Shame on those teachers who force conformity on their followers and who require them to think alike; taking away their God-given ability to make moral decisions based on their own light of faith and reason. If God's living spirit dwells within the minds of men then that spirit must be respected and thus each individual's freedom must also be honored.

If we believe in God, then we must honor him by disallowing religious coercion and forced conformity wherever it is found. Of course the mores will always come into play and social pressure will always be a factor in religious life, but it cannot be the final factor. Religious liberty means more than the ability to choose among varying creeds. Religious liberty is at the heart of freedom. Men either choose to seek God and forsake self, or they choose to forsake God and elevate self. This is the very essence of freedom.

No one can force another to love. Conformity is no antidote to sin and forcing conformity is a sin in itself.

- 10 -
Spirit Dwells in the Mind of Man

EARLIER, I complained of the reticence of my fellow conservatives to employ the word "spiritual." The reason for this, or so I am told, is that when someone says, "I'm not religious, but I'm spiritual," what that person actually means is, "I am a political liberal." He identifies himself as belonging among those who display a "non-judgmental" attitude toward his fellows (in most circumstances) and regards this attitude as the highest social virtue. He exalts the liberation from moral restraint as being, in fact, the highest morality. To the conservative mind, this signifies the renewal of anarchy and decent into barbarism.

Conservatives, in all likelihood, wouldn't be caught dead in a New Age bookstore. But in between the incense, the crystals and the dreamcatchers, some books may be found which are in fact valuable to the personal life of the spirit.

The problem with both sides, the one using the word "spirit" in error and the other refraining from using it at all, is that a word symbol which denotes an entire level of reality has essentially been abandoned. It signals the ultimate triumph of nominalism, for aspects of the spirit are first deemed to be nothing more than mental categories for descriptive purposes and eventually deemed altogether illusory. Both liberals and conservatives buy into this paradigm. Love is now routinely described as a chemical reaction in the brain, not as anything real in itself, much less as an aspect of reality, let alone the *source* of reality. Beauty is deemed to be found "in the eye of the beholder," truth to be subjective, and goodness nothing more than a relative description. A good movie may be worth watching, but it is not good in the same sense St. Francis of Assisi was good. The latter meaning is gradually being lost.

Nowadays, people strive to be successful or to be rich or both, the latter being seen as the measure of the former, but they seldom strive to be good. "That and a dime will buy you a cup of coffee" was how the cynical pre-inflationary saying went. Words like grace and dignity and the states of being they describe have simply been swept away—they won't heat the house or keep the lights on, so where does their worth lie? The act of storing treasure in heaven is seen as a harmless illusion at best, or the mark of a sucker at worst.

Be that as it may, if there were not "something other" operating in the mind of man guiding him toward higher moral aspirations, he would calculate his self interest down to the half-penny in a way even the most ardent evolutionists do not imagine. But that is not the way normal minded people behave. Moral feeling goes all the way down to the essence of what it is to be human.

Those who are spirit-led are not necessarily, or even usually, religious conformists. And therefore it is not the decline of religious institutions that explains the general decline in morality. It is rather the reluctance to acknowledge, much less explore, that realm of reality broadly described by the word "spirit."

Spirit cannot be quantified, because it is quality. It cannot be perceived by the senses, and yet it is sensed. It can be described using the words, beauty, truth, goodness and love. All those who take part in the mystery of existence, perceive the reality described by those words. It is that inner perception which allows us to measure those qualities in the outer world; and it is spirit that breathes creativity into the human mind.

There is an innate goodness within human beings, but it must be acknowledged, cultivated and acted upon to become a living part of a man. He is ever free to reject the guidance of the spirit and to cultivate selfishness to the point of iniquity, to seek fame by shooting up a crowded movie theatre, perhaps, or to strangle a child because his crying has become too bothersome. To become evil is easy, but to become good requires an eternity of effort and determination to substitute a higher will for one's own. It requires constant striving to live in the presence of higher reality.

True religion seeks to perfect man, to make him better and nobler than he is. False religion molds itself to man's lower nature and indulges his appetites. True religion calls man to be more than he is, false religion tells him he's already perfect and it is the outer world, rather than the inner life, which must be altered.

Man is a finite, mortal creature living within a finite and time-bound creation, but that does not mean he cannot glimpse that which is eternal and infinite through spiritual experience—living religion. Conservatives should think twice before substituting religious cultural forms for that very experience and liberals should think twice before throwing out the living truths contained within those ancient forms by focusing exclusively on experience.

Nevertheless, there is a great deal of difference between knowing God and trying to work out all the whys and wherefores about God by using reason. Many people, perhaps most, are too busy to bother with God. To know God requires spending time with him, but it is certainly no more a mystery to know God than to know any other personality. He is as available to the humble and unlettered as he is to the intellectual and learned. The experience of God's presence is solely dependant upon spiritual capacity and this is entirely separate from intellectual capacity. God is no respecter of persons—a fact which should give all sincere seekers pause.

Once God's presence is known, however, then his omnipresence becomes self-evident. The God knowing person sees God everywhere. Truth, beauty and goodness become part of life's everyday experience and one may be said to have entered the kingdom of heaven or to have experienced Nirvana, at least temporarily. There is nothing left-wing or right-wing about this. Religion and religious concepts must not be enslaved to mere political ideas which are as changing as the seasons. Religion is the property of all mankind.

A commentator in Werner Herzog's excellent documentary, *Cave of Forgotten Dreams,* suggested that humanity would be better designated as *Homo spiritus* rather than *Homo sapiens* because it is evident that early man was at least dimly aware of a reality greater than himself and was inspired to create art and religious forms.

The fine drawing below was completed some 30,000 years before Christ walked the earth. The man who drew it was forced to contend with lions, woolly rhinoceroses, wild horses and mammoths from his cave in ice age southern France. The cave where this painting was found also contained a bear's skull carefully placed on a kind of stone altar and the footprint of a wolf or dog beside the footprint of a boy.

There is no doubt these people were transcendent over their environment, not simply functioning as part of the ecosystem like other animals. They were evaluating their reality and thus demonstrating transcendence operating in the mind of man. That transcendence is referred to as *spirit* and it is spirit which makes us human.

— Prehistoric cave painting from the Chauvet-Pont-d'Arc Cave in the Ardèche department of southern France.

- 11 -
The Real Nature of the Soul

FOR MILLENIA mankind has referred to the soul as a human spiritual entity destined to survive the death of the body. Progressive religious experience includes the consciousness of this growing inner reality, something which is born and which develops within. Like a grain of wheat within the husk, which, after the threshing (death), that grain (the soul) is gathered into the barn (heaven) and saved. The husk (the body) is then good for nothing, but to be bound together and burnt, that is, to be returned to the elements from which it came. It is the soul which has value, the soul which is saved. This basic narrative has been fairly universal and constant over the centuries, though it has been thought that the body must be resurrected as a vehicle for the soul's continuance in many theological systems.

Those who confidently assert that the soul is simply a "myth" must answer the question as to why so many people are willing to testify as to the existence of their souls living within them today and how that experience extends back as far as there is written history to record it. The religions of man have long recognized that there was something in addition to the divine spirit living within human beings. In ancient Egypt we find the concept of the *ka* (the spirit — though at first only kings were thought to be touched by the divine and to be in possession of a *ka*) and the *ba* (soul) just as the *yin* and *yang* are found in ancient China in a similar relation.

The soul may be understood as the offspring of the mortal mind and the divine spirit. When the Father bestows personhood upon the human animal, he creates a center of gravity—a force for integrating and harmonizing the systems of matter, mind and spirit into one being. The mind may be envisioned as resting upon the electro-chemical energies of the brain below and impinging upon spiritual energies above. During life, we are entirely unconscious of the electrical sparking of the neurons and the effects of various hormones acting in the brain below, likewise, are we mostly unconscious of the activities of the spirit above. What we are conscious of is mind itself. And within mind there are roughly three levels, the unconsciousness or the sub-conscious (the level of mind closest to the body), the conscious, and the super-conscious (the level of mind closest to the spirit).

It is through our decisions, first to know God, and then to follow his moral leading, thus becoming more and more self-identified with spirit, that the soul is first born and then grows increasingly real during our lifetime. The soul is thus the embryo of our future state. Personhood, along with its prerogative of will, remains the center of gravity within the soul. When the physical body dies, the soul remains and I am convinced that memory, or at least memory most valuable to the continuation of personhood, also remains and is transferred to a new existence.

A major flaw in the idea of reincarnation is the lack of memory continuity. There is also a question as to whether memory is actually stored inside brain cells or whether the brain simply plays a part in memory retrieval. I think the latter much more likely. Memory properly belongs to mind which is non-material.

It is the soul which perceives and responds to spiritual value, that is, Truth, Beauty and Goodness. When, for example, one listens to a beautiful piece of music, what occurs is more than mere sensory perception, intellectual understanding or emotional empathy. The soul perceives and responds directly and the listener is *changed*. Values are always profoundly *felt*—they are not sensory perceptions or intellectual conclusions, they are experiences of the soul, religious experiences.

Modern scientists, in their mad rush to reduce all reality to matter, continually skip over basic questions as though they were unnecessary. For example, the "big bang theory" posits the beginning of reality as a gigantic explosion while skipping the obvious fact that spacetime must have been pre-existent in order for matter-energy to exist at all or for an explosion to occur through time within space. Matter cannot create space and time, these had to have prior existence. Thus the big bang, if it occurred, cannot be touted as "the beginning"—not even close. The basic elements of reality were already there (see chapter 16, "Infinity, Eternity and the Absolute").

Likewise, scientists, in rushing to reduce mind to brain matter, forget that all sensory experience, including scientific observation, exist as phenomena of the mind. Not only are the scientific observations occurring in the mind of the scientist, but the connections between those observations which denote meaning are most assuredly occurring in mind and in mind alone. Using mind to try to disprove the reality of mind is pointless at best and fraudulent at worst—likely an astonishing feat of self-deception as well.

Confidently assertive though they may be, our scientists seem to have become hopelessly lost in the weeds and are now in the position of denying basic reality just as did the Medieval Church.

When Galileo testified to his experience of witnessing mountains and craters on the moon through a telescope, the Church was put in the position of either having to deny his experience (and that of others) or to broaden its philosophy. Science must now broaden *its* philosophy to include the non-material or it will eventually lose the fundamental respect of the common-sense populace, especially since the standard Darwinian explanations for the human condition consistently trivialize human life and the human moral struggle, formulating conclusions that are so shallow as to be laughable. For example, that the reason people prefer water and trees in landscape painting is not because they are inherently beautiful, but because water and shelter are necessary for survival.

This by no means implies we should return to the age of miracles, or of doctrinaire, unyielding religious dogma, but is rather a plea to acknowledge the reality of the religion of experience. Just as the early scientists argued that doctrine cannot deny experience (specifically, observation and experiment), neither should a scientific materialistic doctrine deny the plain fact of the everyday human experience of the non-material—specifically of mind and soul. Ultimately, all experience is translated within the mind and soul and both of these are non-material phenomena. Man does not exist as matter alone.

I know my soul exists in the same way I know the desk on which I write these words exists—I experience it. Spiritual experience and divine assurance are the essential ingredients for lasting happiness, a happiness material philosophy and material pursuits can never and will never provide. The pursuit of righteousness and the growth of virtue are not the delusions of a child-like mind in fear of death, but rather the robust exercise of faith by a balanced and mature human being. Character growth is real, mind is real and the evolution of the soul is real. It is rather those who deny the reality of these things who are pursuing an illusion, and in doing so, would trap man in perpetual immaturity by denying the reality of higher values as well as the reality of mind with which he may pursue them. Philosophy and theology, must eventually transcend doctrine, and even Reason, as it too is often limited by doctrine, and finally give way to the reality of experience.

- 12 -
The Unfolding Self

*Nothing is so important to a man as his own state,
nothing is so formidable to him as eternity; and thus
it is not natural that there should be men indifferent
to the loss of their existence...*
— Blaise Pascal *Pensées* #194

*[T]he torment of despair is precisely the inability to
die...he cannot consume himself, cannot be rid of
himself, cannot become nothing. This is the height-
ened formula for despair, the rising fever in the sickness of the self.*
— Søren Kierkegaard, *The Sickness Unto Death*

I T SEEMS to me there is present in modern humanity
a growing ambivalence towards living. Suicide is
now the primary cause of injury-related death in the United
States and this urge to embrace death is steadily rising. Parallel to this, there seems to be a growing tendency to want to
remake ourselves as other people—younger, better-looking,
different. Advancing technology and medicine are allowing

us to play out our fantasies like never before, and yet we cannot be rid of ourselves, we cannot become different persons no matter how much we may pretend or wish to be so.

Incredibly, we find ourselves marooned upon a small island of reality bracketed by a profound and unknown eternity. We don't know why we are here in this place and time, yet in pondering the question of existence, the possibility of something more, some greater purpose, certainly arises. Still, many people seem entirely willing to toss away the opportunity for eternal life (just like the old woman at the end of the movie *Titanic* who dropped her priceless gem into the sea—plop, gone, lost forever), without a second thought. How shall we view this unseriousness toward ourselves and our destinies? Certainly it is a symptom of the decline of civilization that our culture is not providing people a reason to go on living, let alone a reason to cultivate our inner lives in hope that something real will live on in a future existence.

Reality as we know it seems to be one great dynamic process of the potential becoming actual. The potential for the tree is in the seed, the potential for water is in the molecules of hydrogen and oxygen, the potential for the growth of the soul lies in the combination of the material and the spiritual in human experience.

For the mortal man with immortal aspirations, the concerns of this life tend to fall away as the concerns of the next life, of securing one's place in the next life, loom large. When life is looked upon in this way, what does it matter if one lives during times of civilizational vigor or decline? What does it matter if nations rise or fall? From the eternal viewpoint, life is a testing ground, and is never seen as the sum total of reality.

We are pushing through the dirt and muck of this life in order to reach the sunlight which is almost hidden above. It is easy to lose our way and to move toward the depths, but those who strive to convince others that the way toward darkness is just as life sustaining as the way toward light, should not be given credence. We are tired of death and destruction. Eternal life is not only possible, but once that possibility is admitted, it is everything. Nothing else in human experience can compare to the stakes at hand.

We did not create ourselves and we cannot uncreate ourselves. We can be envious and covet that which others have and what they seem to be, but we cannot change who we really are or the potential we alone hold within. All we can do is cooperate in the gradual unfolding of our potential. And just as a tree grows more branches so that more leaves, buds and fruit may appear, the more we actualize our inner potential, the more we grow in potential. "For to everyone who has, more will be given."[1]

In a sense, our mind and will are the stewards of our eternal selves and so the duty we owe to our creator is found in the development of our true natures, the multiplication of our "talents," according to the parable. We must cooperate in our own becoming, the process of releasing our eternal potential into actual being. This process involves a willingness to be led and directed by our highest moral perception, no matter the material consequences. It involves the process of embracing oneself and accepting all the aspects of one's own being and entails the effort to cultivate our true talents, however small and insignificant they may seem to be at first. The slow and often painful process of personal growth cannot be bypassed. However much we may want to skip ahead and be now what we have not yet become, time must intervene. The way of the universe is slow, but sure. All growth requires time and we are creatures of time. Our potential unfolds slowly over the course of our lives and this unfolding will continue eternally if we so choose.

---

1 Matthew 25:29.

The atheist will say, I have no duty to God, rather, if there is a God, he has a duty to me. The believer feels gratitude for his existence, even in suffering, and seeks to find his duty to God. The believer will seek first to find and then to do the will of God, he will seek higher motives to replace lower ones, he will seek an ever higher morality and he will seek to do that which is right even in the face of complex emotion and conflicting feelings. He will lay down his will and his life for a greater will and a greater life—he must give all that he has in order to become more than he is.

There is no easy way to enter eternal life. For every person, the cost is steep, very steep indeed, and it will never be less. "Again, the kingdom of heaven is like treasure hidden in a field, which a man found and hid; and for joy over it he goes and sells all that he has and buys that field."[2]

The cost of entrance is sometimes one last secret sin which must be placed upon the scale. One might possibly do hundreds or thousands of good works, but without that final sacrifice, small as it may be, the door will remain locked.

Eternal life has to be the thing desired above all else. There is no way around the cost, the cost is all men really have, the only thing of value to God, and that is our will. When we give our will to God it is not a passive thing. It is not simply a matter of following the rules laid out by scripture. Rather, the seeking and doing of God's will is dynamic and all encompassing. We give God not only our actions, but our thoughts as well. We allow him to enter our minds and to alter our thoughts. There is no hiding, there can be nothing held back, and there is no going back once that threshold is crossed.

Thereafter, one may feel like a stranger in a strange land—a sojourner on earth. But it is incumbent upon all those who have seen the promised land to become thereafter

---

2 Matthew 13:44.

ambassadors of that land and to represent it to their fellows who have yet to see it. The end of the earth is not dust and death. There is a place where all things of value are saved, where the wheat is separated from the chaff, that is, where the real is separated from the unreal. This has been called the kingdom of heaven but it might also be called the kingdom of permanence, the kingdom of the real.

- 13 -
The Reality of Faith

Now faith is the substance of things hoped for, the evidence of things not seen.

— Hebrews 11:1

I T IS INTERESTING to note that people who have never experienced real faith, often mistake faith for a kind of hope, and an irrational hope at that. To them, faith seems a very fragile thing, apt to crumble in one's hands the way hope often will. Faith, they believe, is simply a wishful attitude and nothing more.

But those who have experienced faith know it to be more, much more, than mere hope. Faith is the living spiritual connection between oneself and one's creator. It is the result of complete trust and unconditional devotion to a loving and personal God—a being who is goodness personified. Belief in God the Father is not faith, but belief may reach faith levels when it dominates one's thinking so much that it molds one's life entirely. The overwhelming conviction arises through faith that God is that something, or rather someone, for whom life is absolutely worth living and faith assures us that all our pain and striving has an eternal purpose, even that a great destiny may await on the other side of the veil of death for which this life is merely a preparation.

Faith banishes that paralyzing fear that perhaps we have placed our hope in a fleeting shadow or that all our life and work might, in fact, have been in vain. Faith removes fear and fear, more than anything else, is the great obstacle of life. For this reason alone, one would think faith would be assiduously courted by all.

> *Then fear drove out all intelligence from my mind.*
> – Ennius in Cicero, *Tusculan Disputations*, iv. 8.

Unreasoning fear has certainly caused more human anguish than any other emotion. Fear has many times caused normally rational people to commit murder or has driven them to madness or suicide—death being preferable to living with relentless, nameless and fatiguing fear.

On the other hand, a quick perusal of history's most illustrious examples of heroism in the face of pain, humiliation and death (often under physical torture) have been exhibited by man and women of profound religious faith.

Faith is not a product of thought, reason or imagination; neither is it a product of emotion, although hope is connected to both mind and feeling. Faith is a pure spiritual experience and because it is an experience, it cannot adequately, that is rationally, be explained to someone who has never had such an experience. The faithful believer experiences a deep and abiding inner assurance which cannot be given by one person to another and is thus quite baffling to those without it. Nevertheless, faith has been the cement holding families, communities, nations and civilizations together since the dawn of humanity.

Faith is more than knowing, more than believing, more

than hoping God exists. Faith is the experience of God's presence, the assurance of his goodness and the certain reception of the reason for living. Faith is the great channel through which our daily bread is given. Faith is the ladle with which we dip the living spiritual water and refresh our souls. Faith is a muscle which must be exercised in order to grow; the rigors and uncertainties of life actually aid one's faith. (The monastic life may not, in fact, be very conducive to the growth of faith in the hearts of its devotees.)

While prayer gives voice to hope for the future, faith affirms a belief that whatever the future holds is ultimately an expression of the Father's benevolent will, even if that will may be thwarted in the short term by the selfish and unwise acts of his erring children. We may be able to destroy ourselves, even our entire planet, but we cannot destroy the entire universe. Thus, our free will is limited, but it is no less free.

We have the power to set our souls on the path of righteousness, to honor truth, seek mercy and revere goodness, but we cannot save ourselves from the grave. Any hope of eternal continuance of being requires faith, and faith is not the forlorn hope some believe it to be. Faith is active, alive, thrilling and real. Faith is our salvation and faith is the one thing powerful enough to dominate life entirely. That is why, I believe, faith is so often feared and shunned.

Faith grants peace beyond understanding—freedom from fear—and yet, because it is so all-consuming, many intelligent men count the cost and decide they cannot afford to live for something beyond themselves which they cannot see, hear, taste or touch, something beyond their control, something that will, in fact, control them. This is beyond the tolerance of the modern ego-self. But ultimately, who is more deluded: the man who willingly gives control of his life to the great controller, or the one who imagines himself to be in full control? Babies undoubtedly imagine that, according to the law of cause and effect, it is their crying which produces milk.

Neither should one imagine that a life of faith is a life of ease. Nothing could be further from the truth. Faith requires immense effort, both within and without. The greatest men and women of faith have been those of great action. Think of John the Baptist or Joan of Arc. These were not people who shrank from life, but lived lives of faith-filled action and changed history forever with their heroic deeds. Most of us, naturally, are not called to such heights of spiritual demonstration, but we can, each in our station, walk humbly with God and shine his light upon the world to the best of our abilities. It is eternally true that "he who loses his life...shall find it."[1] Faith is that losing and that finding at once—the ultimate liberator.

---

1 Matthew 16:25.

- 14 -
On Forgiveness

I WAS PROMPTED to write on this subject by an
excellent article written by Theodore Dalrymple and
published in *City Journal*[1] in which he discusses an openly
exhibitionist display of forgiveness by a woman named Marian Partington who claimed in her book to forgive her sister's
torture and murder at the hands of a notorious serial-mur-
dering couple, Frederick and Rosemary West. She details
her struggle to forgive Rosemary West specifically, who had
not sought her forgiveness and indeed returned her letters
with a request that Partington cease all correspondence with
her. Ms. Partington nevertheless proceeded to write a book
about her inner quest to forgive Mrs. West, presented, and
no doubt marketed, as climbing the Mt. Everest of forgiveness, for who could forgive a thing like that but the most
forgiving person in the world?

With the collapse of religion, tolerance has been raised
above justice and forgiveness above mercy. Forgiveness of
every wrong along with tolerance of every thing is now the
universal expectation—a marker of being a spiritual person.

---

1 Theodore Dalrymple, "Sentimentalizing Serial Murder," *City Journal*,
Autumn 2012.

Dalrymple describes this kind of "incontinent forgiveness" as a signal of egotism and/or spiritual pride, a kind of spiritual one-upmanship the modern world seems to be engaged in. "I am more spiritual than you are and as proof of this, I have forgiven the most evil person imaginable."

There are several problems with this. First, as Dr. Dalrymple points out, we can only forgive the evil done to us personally, not that done to others. In this case, Marian Partington could forgive her own sorrow at the loss of her sister, but she could hardly forgive the torture/murder itself. Second, in order to forgive someone we must imaginatively enter into the wrong-doer's world to understand his actions. This is hardly possible with actions as evil as that done by the Wests. Thirdly we must understand that those who become habitual evil-doers are highly unlikely to repent or seek forgiveness; indeed, the more hardened they become, the less likely they are to accept any form of forgiveness, from either God or man. In that case, the offer of human forgiveness is simply a futile display of pride, ignorance or both.

Of course, pride and specifically spiritual pride were once universally recognized as sin. You may recall that pride was the great sin of Lucifer.

Fourthly, personal forgiveness cannot be extended to the realm of public justice—the obligation of society to protect and defend the innocent is paramount. Fifth, there is the idea that God is all-forgiving and therefore, the thinking goes, that to be all-forgiving ourselves is to display God-like behavior. The problem with this is that if God were all-forgiving he would be unjust, and if he were unjust, he would not be good, and if he were not good, he would not be God. In the final analysis, God is not mocked.

All that being said; however, it is important for those who seek to move closer to God to forgive those who trespass against them, for this is the key to the personal experience of divine forgiveness.

When we seek divine forgiveness, we seek entrance into the kingdom of heaven and all that goes with it, including life eternal. It is unfair to hold grudges over the small wrongs done to us (often for matters of personal pride) when we seek forgiveness of all our sins and acceptance into the realm of eternal existence. No matter what we forgive, the nature of human forgiveness is a small and insubstantial thing in comparison with divine forgiveness. In this light, it is impossible to withhold our small mite of forgiveness for the same human weaknesses for which we ourselves expect to be forgiven on high.

> Then Peter came to Him and said, "Lord, how often shall my brother sin against me, and I forgive him? Up to seven times?"
>
> Jesus said to him, "I do not say to you, up to seven times, but up to seventy times seven. Therefore the kingdom of heaven is like a certain king who wanted to settle accounts with his servants. And when he had begun to settle accounts, one was brought to him who owed him ten thousand talents. But as he was not able to pay, his master commanded that he be sold, with his wife and children and all that he had, and that payment be made. The servant therefore fell down before him, saying, 'Master, have patience with me, and I will pay you all.' Then the master of that servant was moved with compassion, released him, and forgave him the debt.
>
> "But that servant went out and found one of his fellow servants who owed him a hundred denarii; and he laid hands on him and took him by the throat,

saying, 'Pay me what you owe!' So his fellow servant fell down at his feet and begged him, saying, 'Have patience with me, and I will pay you all.' And he would not, but went and threw him into prison till he should pay the debt. So when his fellow servants saw what had been done, they were very grieved, and came and told their master all that had been done. Then his master, after he had called him, said to him, 'You wicked servant! I forgave you all that debt because you begged me. Should you not also have had compassion on your fellow servant, just as I had pity on you?'[2]

The effect of forgiveness by a human being on the one forgiven varies greatly. The person forgiven may feel such gratitude that his whole life is altered from that moment, or the person may simply mock the forgiver, holding forgiveness as nothing. Rosemary West was not seeking forgiveness. It meant nothing to her.

It seems, however, there is always a noticeable effect on the forgiver himself. Upon forgiving another, people often speak of feeling as though a great weight had been lifted and are conscious of increased spiritual freedom, as if a fresh breeze has blown through their minds, clearing out the old and making space for new spiritual growth. There is also a new consciousness of having been forgiven—a consciousness of God's love. This priceless gem is purchased by giving up pride, for it is pride which holds on to the sense of having been wronged. Pride results from an exaggerated sense of self-importance; it nurses grievances and resentments and these may eventually lead to evil actions. It is fashionable to call this "narcissism" today, as though it were a rare phenomenon. A generation ago, it was called pride and recognized

---

2 Matthew 18: 21-33.

forthrightly as a sin—a sin of which we are all guilty.

Our children are no longer taught these simple truths. Children are naturally egotists. It used to be the role of the home and church to dampen and correct this tendency, but with both these institutions in shambles, many children have no brake upon their sense of self-importance and are easily lured into byways of selfish pleasure, which they themselves no longer recognize as sinful. It is no wonder that the home is in crisis, for home-building requires the sublimation of ego-desires; it requires self-sacrifice and that is not something anyone feels obligated to do anymore. That is why pride in forgiveness of the kind exhibited by Marion Partington is so loathsome: it reveals a twisting and distortion of spiritual value which has become an integral part of the modern sensibility.

- 15 -
The Primacy of Human Will

Behold, I stand at the door and knock. If anyone
hears My voice and opens the door, I will come in to
him and dine with him, and he with Me.

— Revelation 3:20

MATERIAL DETERMINISTS continue to argue that human free will is a cruel illusion. Sam Harris, for example, argues that whereas we are not our own creators, and did not create all the myriad factors of our environment, do not control all the factors of influence that go into our genetic and environmental make-up, that therefore no decision made can be said to have been truly free.[1] All the evolutionary factors of our make-up going back to the beginning of life on earth (indeed beyond, since why this planet and not another?) would have to have been consciously decided by us to make our decisions fully free since all of those factors influence our decisions at least to some degree now. Hence, our decisions are limited; therefore, we are not free

---

1 See Sam Harris, *Free Will*, Free Press, 2012.

will beings.

I would tend to agree with Mr. Harris, if it were true that human beings were merely material constructs with no perception or experience of non-material reality. But that is not true; human beings perceive and act upon spiritual value, we distinguish good from evil, and it is these very decisions which are valuable in and of themselves. Though human beings are built upon an evolutionary animal substrate, and that substrate predetermines many kinds of preferences and desires during material life, nevertheless, the most critical moral decisions are made by distinguishing between levels of value. In this realm, involving the choosing of better and more moral positions among our fellow men, we are completely free. In the absence of mental illness or serious brain injury, both good and evil are freely chosen.

These are the decisions upon which our lives are built. The fact that I like eggs for breakfast, may have been influenced by an omnivorous ancestor in the distant past, but my moral decisions determine my future—what kind of person I will become, what kind of character I will develop and how I will treat others throughout my life. "Love thy neighbor as thyself" is not a formula for survival of the fittest. Moral decisions do not confer survival value in the material world, in fact, they often do the very opposite, but they do enhance survival potential for a life beyond this one in which spiritual value predominates.

Some influential religious thinkers, most notably Martin Luther and John Calvin, speculated that if God were all-powerful, then human life must be predestined. This formula fails to consider the idea that God may have decided to self-limit his power in order that man may have freedom. The great illustration of this is, of course, the death of Jesus. Though he could heal the sick, give sight to the blind and raise the dead, he did not resist his arrest, trial and execution, but rather submitted to the will of man—God's will in voluntary submission to human will. A more powerful demonstration of the nature of God could not be found.

Another demonstration may be easily observed in our own experience with the spirit. We must consciously open the door for spiritual experience to occur and when we turn away, the spirit obediently withdraws. God's spirit does not dominate or control us. It provides comfort, guidance and support, but never coercion. And this must be because the decision was made sometime in the distant past to allow man his free will.

The idea of God being self-limiting is rather obvious. What is time, but the limitation of eternity? What is the finite, but the limited infinite? What is matter, but limited energy? The infinite, eternal and absolute Godhead, must have limited himself in order for creation to begin, for time and space to become real. God may know the end from the beginning, but the getting there may take zillions of different pathways depending on the individual freewill decisions made by his creatures. The Father is probably not surprised by our decisions, but that doesn't diminish the fact that (within an admittedly limited framework) we have made those choices freely.

We choose to love God and we choose to love one another; we cannot be forced to do so. To love another person as ourselves involves a perfectly free choice. It is not enslavement to ritual or belief in dogma, love can only be given freely or not at all. Love is spirit. It is not created by material antecedents.

In order to be free to choose the good, we must be free to choose its opposite—evil; we must therefore be free to sin. Without the possibility of evil, there would be no choice and no freedom. So to the unthinking question, why does God allow evil; the answer is, that we may be free and come to him of our own volition. Those who would remove that freedom and make men slaves are in direct rebellion against God's will and purpose. Muhammad was one such rebel who would enslave men to a ritualistic system, but those philosopher-scientists who would remove man's free will choice by convincing him freedom does not exist (just as God does not exist in their thinking) are rebels in the same way. Both destroy human dignity by destroying human freedom. Both offer nothing but bondage to meaningless forms and the return to animal levels of existence. In the one, man is the helpless pawn of an evil deity, in the other, man is the helpless pawn of soulless matter and consequently any degree of human enslavement is justified on the basis of seeking material well-being for the multitudes.

Communism, of course, was predicated on atheism, but a still more terrible totalitarianism is sure to come with the spreading acceptance of material determinism and its destruction of belief in the reality of free will.

- 16 -
Infinity, Eternity and the Absolute

ACCORDING TO the high priests of our age, our scientists, the present universe was created at a specific point in time, some 13.81 billion years ago, with the explosion of a material "singularity" of infinite density, pressure and temperature which existed within an infinite void. In other words, all matter, which according to these scientists, is the only reality, was compressed into a single, infinite point and then that point spontaneously exploded, distributing matter through space. This undifferentiated and mindless matter immediately self-organized, creating atoms and molecules, stars and galaxies. According to the theory, matter may continue to expand for an eon and then begin to contract again in the "big crunch," forming another infinite singularity which would then repeat the performance over and over throughout eternity. Or, on the other hand, matter may expand forever into infinity.

This assumes two essential things. One is that time is eternal and the other is that space is infinite. I wonder whether either of these premises is justified.

Consider Zeno's formula of the infinite halves. In order for an ant to travel an inch, it must first cross a half inch, and before that a quarter inch, and before that an eighth through an infinite number of preliminary halfway points. If the universe of matter were indeed infinite, the ant could not move forward. The same thought experiment can be done with time—one second must pass, but before that, a half second, a quarter second and so forth through another infinite series. In this case, time could not flow, it would "stand still" and be an eternal moment.

It seems self-evident, to me if to no one else, that time cannot be eternal nor can space be infinite at least on the level of reality we presently inhabit. If they were so, there could be no motion through space and time; there would be nothing at all—nothing material, at least.

Time may profitably be described as limited eternity and space as limited infinity. Both of these limitations must be present before there can be anything other than the Absolute One. As I stated earlier, exploding matter could not create time and space, because time and space had to be present before matter (or matter-energy) could exist and explode within it.

An infinite and eternal reality is not our own. We are time and space limited creatures with very little to guide us to the possible existence of these absolute levels other than mathematics. And of course, the blackboard is the one place where these speculations regularly take place. Infinity is a useful concept in mathematics, but it is hard to see how it could exist in the time and space limited world we actually inhabit.

To take another example, it is generally understood that the Universe, vast as it is, contains a limited amount of matter, so how could a finite amount become infinite through compression alone within the theoretical, primordial singularity? Alternatively, how could infinite singularities exist within black holes if those holes are still adding matter? The idea of infinite density, pressure or temperature may work well mathematically, similar to the "limit" employed in calculus, but it is doubtful as a true reflection of our reality. Logically, the infinite and eternal are the higher level from which space and time are derived, not visa versa. The greater cannot be carved from the lesser. We may glimpse infinity through the prism of mathematics, but it is not something actually observable in spacetime, because it cannot exist within its limits. Matter and energy, space and time are all finite realities, not infinite ones. This is why Einstein's special and general relativity theories both work. Time and space are two manifestations of the same phenomenon (spacetime), just as are matter and energy ($E=mc^2$).

The leap from science to theology is not that far when discussing origins or trying, in other words, to "read the mind of God." And the seldom considered Trinity concept is interesting here, because it postulates three co-eternal and co-infinite beings such that God's first act of creation was to escape his own absoluteness—his aloneness. Will (the Father), thought (the Son or the Word) and deed (the acting Spirit) are all necessary for creation.

The dividing line between philosophy and theology lies in the explanation of why there is something rather than nothing. Theology postulates a primal will, but philosophy is free to speculate that perhaps the ultimate "why" has no answer or to dismiss the question itself as meaningless. For the religionist, however, the world exists because God didn't want to be alone, it exists so that his creatures, especially those capable of will, thought and deed (those made in the "image" of God), might share in creation, might share in the life of God.

Of course, there may be numerous levels of reality in between the spacetime realm of matter-energy and the absolute realm of infinity-eternity. We have no way of knowing, but until armchair philosophy is outlawed, it will still be permissible to wonder.

> The problem involved is too vast for our limited minds... We are in the position of a little child entering a huge library filled with books in many languages. The child knows someone must have written those books. It does not know how. It does not understand the languages in which they are written. The child dimly suspects a mysterious order in the arrangement of the books but doesn't know what it is. That, it seems to me, is the attitude of even the most intelligent human being toward God. We see the universe marvelously arranged and obeying certain laws but only dimly understand these laws.
>
> — Albert Einstein[1]

---

1 From an interview conducted by G. S. Viereck in 1929, quoted in Viereck's *Glimpses of the Great* (Macauley, New York) 1930.

- 17 -
Fearing the Man from Nazareth

S OMETHING THE MOST vehement non-Muslim defenders of Islam often tell me is they have no fear of the consequences of Islamization, either for themselves or for their descendants, whatsoever. The idea of misogynous, homophobic, antisemitic, anti-American communities proliferating on American soil while openly seeking the overthrow of the Constitution is no cause for their concern. They believe Muslim societies can easily co-exist in a secular world, despite ever mounting evidence to the contrary. These people wear their lack of concern as a badge of honor—as evidence of superior tolerance and thus of superior moral sensibility.

Instead, what they often tell me (usually in highly hysterical tones) is that their greater fear—much greater fear—is of Christianity and of Christians.

Buried in this fear is the unrecognized admission that the only thing strong enough to oppose the belief system of Islam (the life and teaching of a seventh century Arab warlord) is its opposite (*i.e.*, the life and teaching of a first century Jewish carpenter). For them, the actual teachings of Muhammad may be safely ignored without engendering inner turmoil, but the teachings of Jesus cannot be so easily put aside—they must take up arms in opposition. And thus they must side with and defend that which they undoubtedly believe to be false, that is, Islam, rather than deal with the simple lessons of the Gospel: that God is good, that morality is real and that death is not the end. This is the true threat to their peace of mind, a threat to everything they think they know.

Indeed, all sincere seekers of truth must eventually grapple with the man from Nazareth and decide for themselves if he spoke the truth or was instead the greatest liar the world has ever known. This is what the enemies of Christianity want to avoid—a personal confrontation with the Nazarene fisherman. It is much easier to throw some lightly considered saying of Jesus back in the face of Christians (on turning the other cheek, for example) than to really delve into the parables or the Sermon on the Mount.

Much has been written about the fact that we live in the afterglow of Christian civilization, that the moral worldview we think of as being inborn is actually an effect of the Christian substructure our civilization is built upon. Nothing makes this clearer than the experience of observing the worldview and moral structure of Islamic belief and Islamic societies. It is a totally different way of looking at the world and man's place in it. The morality of Islam is a complete inversion to Christian morality, the morality we think of as natural with or without Christ.

The real nature of morality has been and continues to be studiously avoided on both sides of the Islam debate. It is easier for many Islam critics to focus on the unjust political side of Islam and pretend that morality and religion are beside the point. As Pamela Geller often says, "I don't care if you worship a stone, just don't stone me with it." Or, Bill Warner: "Religion is what you have do to gain heaven or avoid hell," the implication of both statements being that religious belief concerns no one but the believer and can therefore be safely ignored—only that which is political needs to be dealt with. Politics is something we're comfortable with. Religion is something we think we've left behind, or is something so personal, we're afraid to discuss it in the public arena.

Unfortunately, even in this age of relativism, religion, morality and spirituality must all be dealt with—openly and publicly. All the great conflicts of history have been essentially moral conflicts between two levels of spiritual perception. Those who are unsure of right and wrong have no defense against those who are absolutely certain of the rightness of their cause and the purity of their motives.

Christians are taught to serve God by serving man, Muslims are taught to serve God by serving Islam at the expense of man. Has there ever, in the history of humanity, been a more clear-cut moral difference?

The world our proliferating atheist class would build, one in which there is no God and therefore no moral structure to the universe, could never sustain freedom for long. In that world there is no reason why some men should not tell others what to think, feel, say and do. Where God's will is not thought to exist, there is no brake on human will and no moral restriction on coercion—for one's own good, of course.

On the other hand, if it is understood that God himself respects the free will of his creatures (within a morally structured universe), then and only then, will men consistently respect the free will of other men. Order can be maintained through inner restraint rather than the outward restraint of law and social coercion.

The only way that the present trend toward increasing coercion can be inhibited is through the realization that true morality results not from societal form, but from the guidance and insights originating from spiritual forces within each human being.

Our entire world of finite reality is ultimately dependant upon a greater infinite and eternal reality—the observable universe is but a tiny sliver of the totality of existence. Therefore our personal reality is likewise dependent on something greater and it is this very dependence which causes rebellion in the ego-self. The ego, like Lucifer, demands total freedom—demands the place of God. Those who take up arms against religion want to be dependent on nothing and responsible to nothing beyond their own selfish ego. They demand the impossible: quite simply to take the place of God.

Islam likewise takes the place of God, so its non-religious defenders would rather battle for this totalitarian system of draconian social control than admit the possibility that they may have been wrong, that there is a God to whom they owe their existence, and thus their allegiance. They would rather cling to the delusion of ego-freedom, rather than grasp true freedom by accepting their sonship with God—discovering one's natural place in the universe as a child of God—not as a slave, nor as a subject, but as a child.

Though God in his absolute form is unchanging, his material creation is nothing but change—growth and decay. We have a firm place to stand only when touching that absolute, eternal and infinite being which lives within and whose voice never stops speaking to us, even though we may seldom hear it.

Therefore, religion must also change. We cannot fight an unchanging belief system by becoming mired in the past ourselves, trapped in an unbending doctrine. It takes faith to follow the Master into the future and to expect that his other children will hear his voice and likewise follow him in their own ways. We cannot fight a system that cruelly forces conformity by forcing conformity of another kind—either by enforcing a creed or by indoctrinating children in unbelief.

No man, no "scientist," no "prophet" no "politician" has the right to force conformity of thought, speech or action on free human beings. Forced conformity is immoral because, and only because, God has given us freedom that no man has the right to take away—no man had the right to play God. True religion is the only thing strong enough to protect freedom, and freedom cannot be maintained when belief in God is undermined. The thought-speech slavery of political correctness is but a tiny foretaste of what is to come.

Tolerating injustice is itself morally corrupting, but allowing an unjust system like Islam to take root within the post Christian world will inevitably lead to the kind of moral confusion Bat Ye'or has so ably described as the mental conditioning of *dhimmitude* which precedes the actual imposition of *dhimmi* status by many years. Those who claim we should not deal with Islam in its religious and moral dimension do nothing to prevent this moral confusion. Morality must be clear, but it must also be forward looking; religious understanding must evolve or it will slowly perish, taking freedom with it.

One thing is certain, religion can no longer be safely ignored.

- 18 -
Christianity's Challenge

I T IS AN unfortunate fact that in the view of the non-Christian world, Christianity seems to be supporting all manner of evil because it fosters Western culture which bears a great deal of guilt for harboring politics without principle, industry without morality, science without conscience, liberty which has turned to license and the accumulation of staggering wealth among the very few. As Western Civilization sinks, Christianity is sinking with it. The most recent Pope's answer often seems to be to embrace the great secular ideal discussed previously, that the highest moral value is non-judgmentalism and thus to participate with the world and its sin; but at least that way the church will not simply become a relic of the past, it may remain at least somewhat relevant.

Certainly the Medieval Church bears primary responsibility for the great reaction against it which resulted in the splintering of the faith into a multitude of sects and the rise of atheism. Indeed, the church begat the modern secular world. Now, it seems the Catholic Church and the myriad Protestant churches will no longer stand in opposition, nor even in contrast, with modernity; they seem intent to simply lose themselves in it.

One cannot, of course, easily discount such a mighty and moral religion as Christianity, set in motion by the handful of followers of a crucified carpenter. This powerful faith conquered the entire Roman world and then went further and conquered its barbarian conquerors. A religion this potent, which absorbed the best of Hellenic philosophy and the Judaic religious tradition, will no doubt resurrect itself and conquer the whole world in time. The Reformation was such a resurrection, but it was also a correction—a rediscovery of the word.

For Christianity to once again recover its submerged strength, Christians of all persuasions must look to the life and teaching of Jesus himself and examine the foundations of the Christian tradition with new eyes. For too long Jesus has been portrayed as meek to the exclusion of his courage. He has been portrayed as a victim to the exclusion of the greater meaning of his life and he has been portrayed as giving the world an unrealistic proposal on which to base man's life—a pleasant fairy tale, no more.

I believe that if young people were introduced to the Master's message in its undiluted form, they would unhesitatingly embrace it and would not falter in carrying it through to the very end. They have been shown a faded cardboard copy of the man; a deeper and more meaningful presentation of Jesus' life and work is needed, one focusing less on the fact of his life (the babe in the manger and the martyr on the cross) and more on the full grown man. Jesus was a man who stood forcefully and steadfastly for magnificent truth. He was a man who feared no man.

First and foremost, modern religion must not be an affront to reason and secondly, its morality must be of the highest order, unconfused by the superstition and paganism of the past. The ancient anthropomorphic God who was jealous, vengeful and unjust, who demanded sacrifice and suffering and found pleasure in the same, must finally be left behind, acknowledged as a stage of religious development, but no more.

The message of Jesus has been coccooned for two millennia. It has been encapsulated in an ancient religious idea—that God requires blood sacrifice in order to appease his wrath and bring forth his forgiveness. This idea is entirely unworthy of enlightened men.

Jesus remains our savior, but not so because of his death, rather, he is so as a result of his exemplary life. Jesus demonstrated, as has no other person before or since, the thrilling adventure of living a life in complete faith and trust in God. He elevated man's relationship with God to the highest point of religious expression and he did so by example.

The meaning of life is found in the effort to live by ones' highest ideals—to live the will of the Father in Heaven by finding justice and truth, goodness and beauty, not as philosophic abstractions, but as living realities in daily life. Theology may define faith, but Jesus lived faith. "Follow me" said he, "I am the way."[1]

We cannot follow Jesus through merely understanding or expanding upon a philosophic formula, especially one concerned mainly with the fact of his death. We follow Jesus by living lives dedicated to doing the will of our Father in Heaven—just as he did. We find our path first by loving God and then by living lives of loving faith-trust, by allowing God to hold us securely in his love. Then we can hold fast to truth and elevate our devotion to morality for we know for certain that the Father will not let us fall. The hunger to live by righteousness and to know and experience living truth only grows brighter and more real with time. To

---

1 John 14:6.

know God as an ever present living reality, the way Jesus did, becomes our goal.

The idea that the blood of the Lamb washes away our sins portrays too much paganism, reflects too much magic and barters too much superstition to uphold the mighty religion of Jesus anymore. The great lesson of the cross must be that God will not interfere in the free decisions of human beings, not that God required the suffering of his innocent son to appease his anger over the state of sinful humanity. God allowed the decisions of all those who sought the death of the Son of Man to be made freely. God does not force man to turn to him, to love him or even to recognize him. God allows man his sin because he allows man his freedom. Our freedom must be worth the terrible price we have paid for it—when generations pay for the sins of previous generations on down the ages.

This is a more difficult message to be sure. Men want certainty; they want to be given the magic words or the magic formula by which their entry into the kingdom is assured. If they could purchase that entry with gold, they would—indeed, many try. How much easier is that than the difficult chore of finding God's will—unique for each man alone—and then of carrying it out, actually doing the will of God. It is a difficult, but not impossible task. God may be found and his will may be discerned. That is what it means to follow Christ.

God's will is the absolute focal point of justice, mercy, goodness, truth and beauty within the soul. How are we to find his will except by searching within? How do we find him but to seek our deepest understanding of morality, our highest discernment of truth? None of this is easy. Often it entails making enemies. Not everyone will understand the effort to live up to one's highest ideals, nor will they understand one's turning away from or even denouncing those who seek a lower road. The lower road is easy to justify and those who stand apart often seem intolerant, inflexible and self-righteous. The cost of following God's will is usually not one big thing, but many, many small things.

Was Jesus concerned about pleasing men? Did he not warn his followers about counting the cost? It is time for institutional Christianity to also count the cost. It can take the easy road and adopt the less demanding morality of modernity—non-judgmentalism—or it can humble itself and kneel before the cross it has so valiantly extolled in times past. Pope Francis was correct when he said, "Tradition and memory of the past must help us to have the courage to open up new areas to God. Those who today always look for disciplinarian solutions, those who long for an exaggerated doctrinal 'security,' those who stubbornly try to recover a past that no longer exists—they have a static and inward-directed view of things. In this way, faith becomes an ideology among other ideologies."[2]

Finding living faith means embracing radical freedom. Is Christianity ready for that?

---

2 From "An Interview with Pope Francis," *New York Times*, September 19, 2013.

- 19 -
The Religion of Experience

THERE IS nothing so formidable as the reality of religious faith. That is why men have sought to tame, harness and control religion throughout human history. The simple message of salvation through faith has never been left alone for long. Man has consistently tried to create human conditions by and through which the believer may be vouchsafed eternal safety. Rituals were introduced, various restrictions and taboos imposed, sacrifices required and a priestly caste enriched—all to create stipulations for salvation, conditions which may be humanly controlled in the never-ending comedy of men seeking to acquire the prerogatives of deity.

Nevertheless, there comes a time in the life of the spiritual seeker when his own experience transcends any consolation or sense of well-being that tradition or ritual may have previously provided. The verity of religious experience naturally becomes one's central reality while ritual and dogma inevitably fall away like scaffolding before a building. These are no longer needed because the certainty of God's actual presence has eclipsed all the steps which helped to bring the seeker to that point.

Nothing can compare with the thrill of knowing God, of discerning his will and endeavoring to carry it out. The certainty of salvation comes not through adherence to law, observance of ritual, sacrifice, tithing or good works. Only through the power of living faith does one become certain of eternal life and this certainty is the most powerful transforming reality known to man. Once one is certain of one's place in the eternal kingdom of God, certain of God's overshadowing watch care, then fear steadily vanishes into the primal mists from which it came.

As I've said before, it is fear which constitutes the greatest stumbling block to happiness and achievement—fear which paralyses action. Religious faith unifies and integrates the entire personality and directs one's energies toward ever heightening ideals. Divided loyalties, and the stress and psychic disruption they cause, gradually pass into the past. One's whole self becomes focused on one objective: the doing of the Father's will and that alone. Perspective is gained as the ups and downs of daily life, even major catastrophes, seem to shrink in significance as one raises one's eyes to take the long view of life, even looking into the eternal and the greater destiny which lies ahead.

The salvation man attains through faith is not only salvation from the ultimate cruelty of the extinction of death; rather, the experience of salvation is multilevel and its fruits are tasted in the mortal life as it is lived now. Through faith, salvation is attained from emptiness and despair, from self-deception and the attempt to inflate self-esteem. We attain salvation from the paralysis of fear and the suffering endured through personal isolation. We attain salvation from self-absorption and experience the joy of losing oneself in service to others. Faith grants salvation from self-destructive impulses. We even attain salvation from ugliness as the beauty of reality begins to dawn in our consciousness. For as fear dissolves away, much that may have seemed repulsive is revealed in its true beauty and harmony of form and color. Observe the marvelous life of insects, for example, the intricate world of those tiny, previously despised creatures engenders awe upon close inspection. Faith even brings salvation from oppression as the discovery of God's guidance delivers us from social pressure to conform to convention or to bend belief to the tyranny of creed.

The constant adjustment made in decisions and one's reactions to the innumerable challenges of daily life constitute the real test of faith. The modification of one's actions and thoughts to reach for ever higher ideals reveals the truth of the growing soul and this is the mark of religious living. True religion is active and dynamic. There is no resting on one's laurels for the truly faithful—only continuous striving for an increasing approximation of perfection of thought, word and deed. And it gradually dawns on the believer's expanding consciousness that there is no end to this striving, for there is no end to God. Finding him is one thing, but getting to know him is a never ending quest.

It is inspiring to ponder, that as we live in him, so does he live through us. As we experience God, he is also experiencing a measure of reality through us. We provide him a unique perspective, the experience of a unique aspect of his creation, something precious and irreplaceable to him. Each human being is uniquely valuable to God and once this is grasped, the brotherhood of man comes sharply into focus—no longer a platitude, but as a living reality. It is this experience, this invisible church, which binds believers together.

Salvation through faith, that is, the actual experience of feeling the assurance of eternal life through God's love which is inexplicably registered in the mind and stamped indelibly upon the heart, trumps all philosophic argument and reduces all ritual and religious form to child's play.

But when that which is perfect has come, then that which is in part will be done away.

When I was a child, I spoke as a child, I understood as a child, I thought as a child; but when I became a man, I put away childish things. For now we see in a mirror, dimly, but then face to face. Now I know in part, but then I shall know just as I also am known.[1]

That knowledge of salvation as attained through faith—living faith in our perfect creator—is ultimately all we need. Only through faith is the personhood of God experienced. Only through faith can man actually approach God. Ritual, dogma and creed are not necessary and even if they may provide helpful intermediary steps toward living faith, they themselves are not faith.

Faith is not material nor is it merely philosophical; it is purely spiritual. Faith cannot be governed or limited by any human agency. Faith is a personal experience of God and with God. It is the open door no man can shut. Reason and philosophy may point toward God, but only faith leads to God. And this simple message, buried under centuries of tradition, philosophy, ritual and dogma, will surely be enough to revive our now sorely weakened civilization. Let the good news be proclaimed: Faith in the living God is all we need.

1 1 Corinthians 13.

- 20 -
The Spiritual Ascent

*[M]y body falls down without pushing, my soul does
not go up without pulling; ascension is my soul's pace
and measure, but precipitation my body's. And even
angels, whose home is heaven and who are winged
too, yet had a ladder and go to heaven by steps.*

— John Donne (*Devotions Upon
Emergent Occasions*, II)

I T IS GENERALLY understood, as Christ taught, that
once one accepts God's grace through a child-like
faith, then he may enter the kingdom of heaven. But it
should be obvious, too, that no one can remain as a child
forever. All of us must grow up and fulfill our duties as adult
spiritual beings. There is no magic wand to relieve us of the
responsibilities to live according to righteous virtue and increasingly to reflect the truth in the widest circumference
of our understanding. The journey does not end with the
consciousness of salvation—it only begins there.

Those who say, "I am saved and will never fear sin,"
are deluding themselves and may fall into the trap of gradu-

al justification of that which originates in their own hearts. Too often men claim to be part of an elect few who can and do transgress the divine will, even flagrantly, in the name of God. Claiming to be of God's chosen, Joseph Smith decided he would marry more than one woman, and that his followers could do likewise, sending the rights of Mormon women back thousands of years. He let himself think that his will and God's will were one and the same.

One need only ponder the fate of Lucifer to know that even those beings created far above the mortal state are not immune to sin. Until such time when our meager souls merge with the divine spirit, so that our very beings, our wills and our souls are one with God, sin will always be latent and this potential is ignored at our peril.

The spiritual journey is marked by periods of both struggle and rest (the consciousness of attaining a new level of spiritual stasis). We do not move to the next level without difficult decision-making. Though it is true we do not save ourselves, it is also true we do not progress in the kingdom without effort and purpose—the higher nature overcomes the lower only by degrees. I do not claim to know how things are in heaven, but I doubt we magically become perfect simply by passing over the threshold of death. Would the Father, having placed within us boundless curiosity and driving ambition, leave us with nothing but endless ennui following death? Would the Father, who has created numberless galaxies, provide no where for us to go, nothing for us to do and nothing more to learn for all eternity?

If we accept that as we progress in the spirit, we simultaneously grow toward God and become more like him, that is to say, more nearly perfect, and if we further accept that God's general plan enables slow, gradual progress (as in physical evolution), then it would be only logical to assume that our spiritual progress continues into the eternal future—we can never completely become God, but we can draw ever closer by infinite degrees until as Donne declared:

> I shall be so like God, as that the Devil himself shall not know me from God, so far, as to find any more place, to fasten temptation upon me, as upon God, nor to conceive any more hope of my falling from that kingdom, than of God's being driven out of it; for, though I shall not be immortal, as God, yet I shall be as immortal as God.[1]

The process of self-identification with God consists of the gradual replacing of old attitudes and old viewpoints with those of a higher reality—to see the world through God's love—all things becoming new. The believing soul is a soul in motion—a soul growing and yearning to grow, even though growth brings pain. Every time the better way is chosen, the lesser way flings up its recriminations and regrets. One can't choose that which is higher unless one recognizes that which is lower and consciously turns away from it. It is easy to behave like a child in the name of spirituality and seek unrestricted self-will. It is easier to pretend that nothing we do is really wrong, but that way madness lies. Self-mastery, leading to spiritual maturity, is difficult. It is a life's, even an eternal life's, journey.

---

1 From a sermon preached before King Charles I in April 1629.

- 21 -
God Descending

JUST AS WE, in our limited ability, ascend toward God, so does God descend toward us, invading and encompassing his entire creation. Though God exists as an absolute, eternal being outside the confines of time and space, there must be some part of God, or level of God, that exists within those self-imposed and self-created confines—a God of time and space. Thus creation remains a part of God, not separate from him. A God of spacetime is required to create, uphold and maintain the Father's vast material creation.

Ultimately of course, God the Father is eternal, absolute and unevolving, but within spacetime, he exists as actualizing potential—he is both actual and potential. Therefore, as we participate in our own self-realization by growing in the spirit, that is to say, as our God-given potential becomes actual in time, we are adding our own small mite to the great actualization of the evolving God. We have been created as unique beings—there is no one else who can contribute exactly the same bit of actualization to God, and thus in a very real sense, God is dependent upon our growth, and our increasing ability to bear the fruits of the spirit, for *his* actualization.

There is a tension in the universe. We are presented with two fundamental ways to become—either to grow toward God and toward reality and thereby to become ever more real in the universe, or, we can reject the divine plan and move away from God and toward unreality, thus becoming more and more unreal until we cease to exist as an active part of the evolving universe—the death from which there is no resurrection. This is the essence of our duty. The great question becomes whether or not we will fail the great soul of creation and defy all that is great and good in the universe by choosing the path of self-destruction. Disloyalty to love and truth carries with it a heavy price.

On the other hand, if we decide to participate in the great evolutionary adventure and to grow toward God, we will not only discover who we truly are in the here and now, but will also begin to glimpse that great immortal being we will eventually become. Once our human will becomes consecrated to doing the will of the Father, our purpose becomes one with God and thus unchanging and eternal. The meaning of life is then found.

As we move through time and mature, we are able to reflect upon more and more of the past and thus project further and more accurately into the future, and by doing so, we evaluate potentials and uncover possibilities. Wisdom and judgment come with maturity and begin to release us from our slavery to the present. When the evaluation of potential is coupled with spiritual insight and guidance, then a higher plane of living is attained and the myriad difficulties of the present are more easily endured. True wisdom is dawning as our mortal minds begin to comprehend deity and we meld our purpose to his.

God the Father sends a part of himself to journey with us through this life. He experiences as we experience and loves his children with us and through us. As we love one another, we demonstrate God's love and fulfill his purpose, our purpose, in life. The real beauty and majesty in life is only discovered through partnership with the eternal God; a God so good he has condescended to come down into our hearts and minds and wait patiently for the tiniest flicker of faith to which he unfailingly responds. Sometimes the onrush of his love is overwhelming, the brightness of his truth is blinding and the realization of his goodness, shattering. And yet, the old ego-self must be shattered if we are ever to find our true, eternal selves.

> Batter my heart, three-person'd God, for you
> As yet but knock, breathe, shine, and seek to mend;
> That I may rise and stand, o'erthrow me, and bend
> Your force to break, blow, burn, and make me new.[1]

If we give God everything we have and are, then he will make us new. That is the Father's eternal promise to his children, but more than that, he will go through the valley of the shadow of death with us. He will descend through time and space to live with us through the extent of this short life and then will slowly and patiently lead us back to Paradise from whence he has come. Let us not fail him.

This is the reality of religious experience and the real nature of religion.

---

1 John Donne, Holy Sonnets 14.